KEEP YOUR SPIRITS UP

KEEP YOUR SPIRITS UP

A Simple Guide to Lift Your Vibes
Sky-high Without Struggle or Pain

MICHELLE PAISLEY REED

Copyright © 2017 by Michelle Paisley Reed

All Rights Reserved

No part of this book may be reproduced, stored in retrieval systems, or transmitted by any means, electronic, mechanical, photocopying, recorded or otherwise without written permission from the author.

Cambria typeface used with permission from Microsoft.

ISBN: 978-1-63161-036-3

Published by TCK Publishing
www.TCKPublishing.com

Get discounts and special deals on our best selling books at
www.tckpublishing.com/bookdeals

Sign up for Michelle's free newsletter at
www.WeAreThePowerOf10.com

I believe there are more urgent and honorable occupations than the incomparable waste of time we call suffering.

~ Colette

To all of our readers and fans from around the world.
We honor and celebrate you and your unique journey.

Thank you!

Contents

Introduction xi
Chapter 1 Addiction to Suffering 1
Chapter 2 Source over Elections 3
Chapter 3 Change Vs. Expansion 7
Chapter 4 Big Picture 11
Chapter 5 Epigenetics 14
Chapter 6 Flow-Let the Power Run Through You 16
Chapter 7 A Leap in Consciousness 18
Chapter 8 From "Me" to "We" Thinking 20
Chapter 9 Allergic to Hypocrisy 23
Chapter 10 Holograms 25
Chapter 11 Prisms 29
Chapter 12 The Afterbirth of the New Reality 32
Chapter 13 Feeling Your Soul 36
Chapter 14 Encoding vs. Decoding 38
Chapter 15 The Easy Way 40
Chapter 16 Hope is a Powerful Emotion 42
Chapter 17 Which Future do You Want to See? 47

Chapter 18 How are You Praying?...51
Chapter 19 We are Not the Only Ones 55
Chapter 20 G.O.D. = Goodness Oriented Direction.................................57
Chapter 21 Don't Change the Channel 60
Chapter 22 All This is Happening So That You May Find Peace............63
Chapter 23 The Universe does not Create Your Authenticity—
You Do..67
Chapter 24 Soul Mates..70
Chapter 25 New Year and Snow 72
Chapter 26 By Being Angry at a Person, You Invite them Further
into Your Experience 74
Chapter 27 Energy Healing will be the ONLY Healing in the Future........77
Chapter 28 Be Careful and Deliberate with your Thoughts
and Actions...79
Chapter 29 From Me to We to Me Again 81
Chapter 30 You All Want Different Things..86
Chapter 31 Source Doesn't Care if You Individuate 88
Chapter 32 Turn Chronic Worry into Joy 90
Chapter 33 If You Don't Believe You Can Fly, You Won't.......................93
Chapter 34 Gilded Everything..95
Chapter 35 The Absence of Resistance is Elation.....................................98
Chapter 36 Taking Inventory...102
Chapter 37 PerSEVERance...104
Chapter 38 Share What You are Learning...106
Chapter 39 Positive Outcome...108
Chapter 40 Man is Frozen 110
Chapter 41 Energy Escalation 112
Chapter 42 Everything Fits Now...114
Chapter 43 Expansion Carries Vibrations Forward 117
Chapter 44 Give Up the Fight..119
Chapter 45 Harmony Can Be Learned...121
Chapter 46 All Wars are Caused by a Lack of Focused Light................124

Chapter 47	When a Soul Lesson is Complete	127
Chapter 48	The Subsequent Ah-ha Moments	130
Chapter 49	A Meditation for You	132
Chapter 50	Finalize the Old Stuff	134
Chapter 51	The Original Meaning of Redemption	137
Chapter 52	Knowing by Heart	140
Chapter 53	You Have Outgrown Contrast	143
Chapter 54	Looking Through New Lenses	145
Chapter 55	Dark Matter	147
Chapter 56	Detachment vs. Disinterest	150
Chapter 57	The Moment of Elation	152
Chapter 58	Everything is as It Is	156
Chapter 59	It's Not Your Fault, but It Is	158
Chapter 60	Money and the Lack Thereof	161
Chapter 61	You Don't Have Anything to Do Today	164
Chapter 62	Believe it Into Being	167
Chapter 63	Wanting Rain and The Law of Propulsion	170
Chapter 64	Raining Creative Opportunities	174
Chapter 65	Opposing Without Hatred	177
Chapter 66	All Movements are Toward Acceptance	179
Chapter 67	Miscommunications and Misunderstandings	181
Chapter 68	Abundance is Expansion in Motion	184
Chapter 69	You Don't Have to Convince Anyone of Anything	186
Chapter 70	Violence = Ignorance + Resistance Amplified	189
Chapter 71	The Opposite Equation	192
Chapter 72	The Less I Personify God and the Universe, the More Empowered I Become	194
Chapter 73	Metabolism	196
Chapter 74	Sensuality and Spirituality	198
Chapter 75	Processing the World Creatively	200
Chapter 76	Approval	202
Chapter 77	Horror	206

Chapter 78 Still and Centered	208
Chapter 79 Be Transparent	210
Chapter 80 Either Way I'll Be Okay	212
Chapter 81 Detoxing from Drama	216
Chapter 82 Scared Shitless	221
Chapter 83 Morals and Aspirations	224
Chapter 84 Alliances	227
Chapter 85 You Are the Miracle	229
Chapter 86 Healing Crisis	231
Chapter 87 Self-service vs. Service of "Others"	234
Chapter 88 Rally for Peace	236
Chapter 89 On Purpose	241
Chapter 90 Peace Party	244
Conclusion	247
About the Author	249
Other Books by Michelle Paisley Reed	251
Book Discounts & Special Deals	253

Introduction

There are now radical numbers of people moving forward toward peace.

You may not always hear about them, for theirs is the collective voice that does not broadcast on negative newscasts.

And yet, you might feel them. After every act of violence, you may join in the lifting of energy toward a higher place that knows no opposite. When we join together in oneness, we realize the higher Truth of who we are, not just who we hope to become.

We are there.

And so, we propose a ratification of the Law of Attraction. While we are not fans of the use of the word "law" as it has negative connotations and implies harsh rules and regulations, there is not yet another word in our vocabulary for "higher Truth." And so, this spiritually evolved state of the Law of Attraction could be called "The Law of Propulsion."

The Law of Propulsion is the Law of Attraction amplified times 10! By now, many of you have been toying with great success employing the Law of Attraction, as well as other man-made "laws" that point the way toward higher Truths. You know that your thoughts create your reality, and yet, you still do not realize that your thoughts are connected with everyone else's thoughts! It is as fun to "lend" your energy to another's manifestation as it is to create your own.

It is as if the density of your bodies has worn you down and slowed you to a pace that might do you harm if not completely ratified.

And so, let's ramp it up, shall we? Are you manifesting so well and so often that you find there is no resistance whatsoever? Are you hoarding your "stuff," or giving freely and sharing with humanity? If you have a pile of stuff, you might want to go back and reread our first two books (*Manifesting Miracles and Money: How to Achieve Peace, Purpose, and Plenty Without Getting in Your Own Way* and *Peace is Power: A Course in Shifting Reality Through Science and Spirituality*). If you find you want to share freely with your global family and bring peace to all, keep reading.

A little more than a year ago, Michelle began receiving our messages and allowing us, at various times, to inhabit her body temporarily to share wisdom from higher planes and perspectives. We are from those higher planes—not so much "higher" as vibrationally faster than where you stand. Because we have chosen not to return to the "learning through hardship" domain, we have a much more rapid frequency—beyond, even, your concept of "heaven," which we see as a stopping-over point (we call it the "way station") on the way to higher, faster dimensions of bliss.

You see, you know by now that your soul is eternal. You know by now that your souls are all one with Spirit, and that Spirit is simply the forward-moving momentum of the Universe. Stay stuck, and you will feel resistance that will make you ill and inhibit growth for everyone. Keep moving, growing, and changing and you will organically move forward in the positive way you were intended to, in that place between lifetimes where you design your storylines for each particular lifetime.

Because we no longer inhabit the entry-level forms of existence known as "bodies" of matter, we are now teachers made of pure Light and Love. We share a common mission to teach, and so our voices are "heard" as one voice, although some of us have chosen to step out from time to time, as we see fit, and share stories and allegories from our old lives. We understand that this may be tough for you to swallow, but please consider the alternative. If you do not start waking up to the Truth of who you really are and where you are really going, you will forever cycle in the learning via suffering game. If you choose to transcend this reality, let us show you how. All you have to do is come from a place of faith and trust.

You are witnessing the polarities apparent in your politics and governments, yes? Those are all just a reflection of who you feel you are as a people—they represent greed and ego, and that is an old state of being, yes?

Once you are ready for a new way of being—and we sincerely hope you are after reading our prior books—we promise to show you how to live it out, to live BIG, to amplify your spiritual powers times 10, so that you may reach a place beyond your current playground and know what it means to live in joy…*all the time.*

Chapter 1

Addiction to Suffering

It is time for humanity to rev up from 0-60mph in 30 seconds.

Michelle recently purchased a brand new sporty car which, because of the seemingly magical circumstances that brought her the perfect vehicle at the right time and at a price she could easily afford, she considers a manifestation.

But we will not get into any manifestation talk right now. If you are not manifesting things, experiences, and opportunities rapidly and frequently, please go back and read our first two books.

The point is, as we have said before, we are here to assist you not just into the next level of your being-ness, but into the fullest expression of your soul. You do not need a thousand more lifetimes to do this—not if you are here now reading this book.

Michelle enjoys her car because it expresses freedom. It is fast—very fast. And so, when she is gearing up to go faster on the freeway, and there are other cars cutting her off by going slower, she simply steps on the gas and goes faster.

The same goes with the people who are populating your planet, many of whom are still what you might call "asleep," but whom we would say are revving at a lower rpm. You are always moving at the cellular level of your bodies, you are always moving and revolving at a planetary level. And so, when you are situated around others who are moving and circulating at a much slower level than you are, it is mandatory to speed things up or die.

That may sound dramatic, but from our perspective, it is the Truth. You came here to evolve, to learn and grow through lessons of pain and suffering. Not an easy path, but one you chose from a place between births of bliss, joy, freedom, and love.

The only thing that gets in the way of your evolution is your addiction to suffering.

True suffering is separation from Source, which is a lie.

You are a part of all that Is, a part of the cosmos—you must know this by now. The greater part of you is universal expansive energy, and when it doesn't keep up with the fast-moving momentum of the entire Universe, the resistance is painful.

Yes, you were meant to learn your lessons. And yes, that's why you came here. But now you may choose an alternate path, one that leads toward faith over fear. Dwell in faith and trust and you can never know fear, for *fear is ultimately an illusion that is attached to a physical experience.*

As you move closer to a place of Spirit, where that greater part of you takes precedence over ego, the ego will fight. Your body will rebel. And yet, over time, Spirit always wins. *Love always wins, although it doesn't seem that way from your physical perspective.* But it does, trust us.

Actually, Love doesn't even need to win. Love always is; Love always exists. It's when you forget this that you get into trouble.

As your ego dissolves—and it will—you will find yourself attaching to other egos' dramas just for old times' sake. It will be painful, and if you are still more attached to ego than Spirit, you will enjoy the suffering. When the suffering is too much, you will stop the madness of learning other people's lessons for them. You just can't.

Chapter 2

Source over Elections

Your Source energy is stronger than any *elect*ion, than any decision.

The most recent American election brought up a lot of fear and pain and uncertainty. Your "leaders" emerged as a reflection of these overall feelings, as nothing ever reveals itself on the greater surface without some participation at the individual ego level.

And so, as the campaigning continued—the cam-PAIN-ing—please look at your choice of words here: you chose leaders who reflected the various levels of greed and ego currently present on your planet.

We say planet here, because it is not just happening in one area of your world, but everywhere on the density of this three-dimensional plane of existence, which is your perception of time and space (that doesn't really exist, but that's another book).

We want you to take a deep look inside and see where you might be reflecting greed and ego. Michelle is writing this on the day after Thanksgiving, which in the U.S. is called Black Friday. There has been a recent trend toward more attention to this day of shopping discounts than to the day of gratitude that precedes it. It is as if the ego wants to skip beyond appreciation for what is, and what it already has, into wanting more and more and more in a never-ending cycle of suffering. For once you buy the trinket, it never fulfills the hole you feel inside. Does it? *How does gratitude feel in you versus attaining an object of your desire?*

You are all living out a hologram of your own making (more on this in later chapters.) Whatever you are experiencing in the outer world is ALWAYS a larger version of what you feel internally—without fail. If you don't like this outer reflection of your society, your world, then do not participate. Without your energetic offering, the reflection goes away. It is as if you were watching a movie on television and you simply turned off the set.

Back to the election. We are *not* advising you not to vote. Notice the double negative within that last sentence. In frequency terms, that sentence read, "We are advising you to vote." The Universe would "hear" it that way if the Universe had ears, which it doesn't. *The Universe, again, is not a person living in the sky.* It is a force of ever-present Love and positive creation. Whatever you say or emote lends itself to positive creation, EVEN IF YOU ARE BEING NEGATIVE.

In this cam-PAIN, there was greater emphasis on what the other person and "party" (another ironic use of the word) was doing wrong than there was on what they intended to enact through positive change. And so, the leader with the greatest energy—good or bad—"won."

Notice, please, the great polarities and division that seemingly appeared after the surprise "win." By now you know that those polarities are an illusion. But those slower-moving bodies of energy do not know this. You see, as they see the apparent derision played out on a larger "screen," they have a greater chance of choosing differently now. Their hologram is reflecting something that—at a greater level—doesn't feel very good because it goes against the greater Truth of their *be*-ing.

How do you stop all this free will derision? *Take a look at your own hologram.* What is the opposite of greed and ego for you? For us, we would say generosity and freedom. Please feel free to insert your own words here, as words are subjective tools of your own perception that only point to the Truth.

If the opposite of greed is generosity, where could you stand to be more generous today? Would it be with your time, or from your pocketbook? What represents giving to you? Do you still wince when you think of giving, as if you are losing a part of you? If so, we recommend going back over our first two books and plan on giving *something* of yourself today, no matter how small.

Michelle opened her pocketbook to give a homeless man two dollars, which was all she had in her wallet. Not only did he graciously accept, but they had a heartfelt exchange of words that made them both rise vibrationally. Connection with other human beings does this. The homeless man—who is just a man, after all—asked about Michelle's new sporty car. In the past, Michelle would feel "guilty" that she had so much while this man apparently had so little. But the greater part of her knew that was not true. The man was admiring the car, and therefore, because we all teach by example, she was giving him inspiration. By looking him in the eye and having a human interchange, she gave him more than those two dollars. And by giving to a man standing out in the cold—by recognizing that the two of them were ONE in reality—she gained far more than the two dollars she gave out.

As you learn to manifest more, it will feel better and better to give out, for through the Law of Circulation, you must learn to give what you receive. Hoarding creates blockages in the mind and body. Your soul is ever-expansive and can always create more, and so as you give you shall receive. Give, give, and give some more, and soon you will see that same level of generosity reflected in those you choose to make decisions for you. Eventually, you will no longer need those leaders to make decisions for you, but that, too, is for a later chapter…or another book. We have said before that your laws and political structures are toppling as you step more into your *true* power, which is freedom. Spirit is freedom, and your soul is part of Spirit, remember?

There are many who would say that your ego is an essential part of you and it will *never* die. We agree—it won't "die." And yet, as long as you affirm that your individuality is necessary, it will be.

We know better. You will always retain higher aspects of personality traits you learned during your various stints on this dense planet. When you reach the space where we reside, do you think that will play any part at all in your bliss? No. That's simply child's play, and of course you will see it as such when you reach higher and higher evolutionary states.

So for now, even your spiritual leaders have told you that you need your ego to survive. And why do you think they said that? They are still human, after all. When they transition into Spirit, they will know the Truth of their expansiveness—as shall you. For now, it is out of the realm of your understanding. You may catch glimpses of this unlimited expansiveness in meditation, but for most people, it makes their heads hurt to contemplate life without an ego.

But it *is* possible, even desirable. In fact, it isn't even desirable, it just *is*—like Love. Just for today, try pretending you have no ego and watch what happens. What does that feel like? Does it frighten you? Do you still have an identity? Or without an identity, do you tend to identify with the greater good?

Chapter 3

Change Vs. Expansion

Your only goal in this lifetime should be to keep envisioning a better version of you.

As you are connected internally to everyone else, when you change *you*, you change us all.

Now to take this even further—as you learn to live your highest and best life, as you tap into the highest and best version of your soul each and every day, you will find that you no longer need to make "changes," per se, because you will expand a little more, just as the Universe does.

Because you are a microcosm of a macrocosmic Universe, in the same way that the cells in your body multiply and amplify to create an adult version of you, your soul also expands and grows—both when you are in Spirit form in between lifetimes, and in your creative dense environment here on earth.

We would like you to think of it as stretching a muscle, as in yoga or another form of exercise. As you allow your soul to stretch to its outer limits, again, you are engaging with the rest of the souls on this planet in the expansion of Spirit, of humanity.

It is, as we have said in previous books, like the Internet in the way you are all connected. Even though you have differing "addresses," you are all part of the great worldwide web, yes? And the same is true of your soul as Spirit. Stop focusing on the address and focus more on the bigger picture. Conversely, as you do the individualized activities that nourish and enrich your creative soul, you expand the whole.

Change may seem scary to most. So please try on the word "expansion" instead. When you are pushing yourself to do more and more and more, it probably doesn't feel good because that is not the way our Universe expands. The Universe doesn't say (because it isn't a person with a mouth), "I want to be bigger and contain more space; therefore, I'm going to push into more and better." That would be silly. Your body doesn't say, "I'm going to push forward into a taller version of myself, and all my organs are going to adapt." It does it on its own, yes? Your body, your Universe, are always in a mode of expansion. Why wouldn't your soul be the same way?

Now the greater part of you that is Spirit, or Source energy, or God—or whatever you wish to call it—is *already* expansive to infinity. It is hard for you to imagine something that is not finite, that goes on and on and on, and yet we are here to tell you that that is indeed the case. YOU go on and on and on because you are part of Spirit.

If that notion feels uncomfortable to you, take that as a sign that you are too attached to the individualized notion of yourself as ego. Remember, ego is just a "role" you signed onto when you auditioned for this play called life. You were cast, and it was a fun role for a while, and you learned a lot about yourself, but then you went on to play a different role in order to highlight your ability to shine differing aspects of your chosen personality.

Michelle and Jodah were speaking of the late (why do you choose that word for "deceased"? No one is late, they are right on time!) American actor Robin Williams and what a varied career he had. He didn't allow his character to be stereotyped into one role. He began as a comic and playing comedic roles, and then showed he could play more serious and dramatic—even scary—roles.

Your soul is the same, you see. Throughout this evolutionary "period," as you chose to come here to create form from energy, you highlighted the dark and the light, the shadow and the shine, in order to form a sort of prism that reflected all sides of you. (More on prisms later.)

You are starting to remember your agreements between lifetimes, aren't you? Do you get glimpses in your dream state? If not, that is not necessary for your soul's evolution. Gather the feelings left behind, not the specific memories.

And when you are done playing your roles out? Like Robin Williams, you just "check out." Now many might get angry with us for saying this, as Williams chose to commit suicide and terminate this particular lifetime early. But we'd like to point out that it was *his* life—his "game"—to end when he wanted to. He just chose to do so more deliberately.

Some might say suicide is selfish. But we'd like to remind you that from where we stand, everything you do is indeed selfish in that you do it to further your own endgame. When someone else opts out, we understand your sadness, as you no longer get to participate with their physical game here on the planet.

And yet, your soul remembers. When you re-enter the non-physical world, your souls will engage magnetically. The energy frequency you emit will be lined up with those who have crossed before you into alternate dimensions—even ours—and you will be reunited. And it will feel amazing.

It can feel amazing right now if you let go of your attachment to people being stuck on earth. It's a challenge, for sure, to realize this. And yet, as part of your reaching into higher consciousness, if you can be aware of people's Spirit selves—whether on the planet or in higher realms of existence—you will always "feel" them. In Truth, of course, you are never really disconnected, as we have stated many times by now.

As you see others as their Spirit selves, you see yourself this way, too, right? It is a much easier and faster way to go to envision the highest and best version of yourself in each new day. What does *she* do, how does *he* behave, how does *she* act, how does *he* dress, how does *she* conduct herself, how does *he* feel? We alternate between gender (pronouns) in the same manner in which you've evolved throughout centuries—*you have all been man and woman, and many of you are beginning to wake up to the fact that it truly does not matter*. Gender, race, ethnicity, religious preferences—they are all just decisions you made pre-birth to experience your soul from different angles. See beyond skin and genitals and region and beliefs to the higher, more expansive version of you, and watch how your life improves for the better. But incrementally—too much at once might be a shock to your system.

As you incrementally improve, so does the whole of humanity and the Universe. Does that excite you? That really excites us!

Chapter 4

Big Picture

Let's look at the big picture for a moment, shall we?

Whatever is going on in your life story, there is an immediate, close-up view, and a broader perspective, yes?

If you were holding a camera on your perceived "situation," whether personal or global, it would look quite different if you zoomed in or out.

Imagine zooming in really close to what is going on around you. You may not need as much drama and contrast to learn as you have in the past, but those near you may still be heavy in the throes of it. *Are you locked into their self-created dramas, or is this your own battle? What if you gave up the battle?*

Even better, what if you realized there is *never* any battle other than the war you wage within you each day.

At the other end of the battle is inner peace. At the other end of inner peace is outer peace—which translates into worldwide peace.

The *only* reason you are not experiencing worldwide peace at this moment is that there is a part of you—obviously the greater part—that does not believe it is possible.

Know that peace *is* possible, in your life and the world you stand on, and it will be so.

Now zoom out. Does the perceived problem in your life look so big at this moment? Does it really even matter? Is it really even yours?

From a global perspective, what we see happening is that the ego is dying.

You may have experienced this process before along your own spiritual path toward self-acceptance and love. When you make changes, all your fears rise to the surface to be healed. You have the opportunity here to sink or swim, to learn a lesson and move forward or stay stuck in your own self-inflicted wounds.

As you move forward courageously in trust and faith, knowing that this is indeed the best way, your ego will fight for your individuality. Those around you might fight for you to stay who you *were*, and not support who you are *becoming*. If you allow those people to drop off your frequency radar, you will rise higher and find a new supporting "cast." It's all a play, remember? If you can remember this whole entire lifetime is a holographic game, you might take it a little lighter and have more fun.

The world is not very fun at this moment of our writing.

Michelle likes to exercise on the treadmill at her gym. Well, "like" is perhaps not the right word, for she only does it to move her body when the weather is cold outside. But as she was walking, she looked up at the many television sets and saw the subtitles that read: "Big changes to transition team."

She knew they were discussing the new American President-elect Donald Trump's news, but as she was focusing on the bigger picture, she had the thought that there are these big changes to the "transition team" all around her!

There are *always* big changes, if you allow and accept them to move you forward. You are *all* in a large state of transition—which many of you call a "shift," and we would call more of a *movement* because of its magnitude—and you, because you are sitting here reading this now, are a part of the team, whether you think you joined it or not.

As part of this "team," it is your mission to welcome change and growth—not the way you've done it in the past through a lot of pain and struggle, but through learning your own lessons through faith and not suffering, and through accepting others for their individual place on the path and *not* telling them what to do, and by loving yourself as much as humanly possible, remembering the love you are between lifetimes.

Tap into that greater part of you now. How does she/he feel? Actually, as you have no gender in Spirit, how do YOU feel? Actually, since you have no ego in Spirit, how does it feel to be immersed in part of Spirit, yet still know who "you" are?

Spend today looking through the big picture lens both personally and politically. Understand that whatever you are going through, the world is going through in its own time, on its own schedule. You control *you*, and no one and nothing else! Do what you do, be as happy and satisfied as you can in each moment, and let others do their own thing. Yes, it is that simple.

Chapter 5

Epigenetics

Scientists are currently studying how to effectively turn "off" the switch for certain types of diseases. This could revolutionize medicine, as not all of your bodily diseases are solely due to your inherited genetic makeup. You also inherited various habits, attitudes, and environmental living situations that your parents chose, but you can turn those "off" *just by deciding to*!

Your bodily health is important. You know this by now, and yet many of you still don't take care of your vehicle. It starts in the mind. You not only make decisions to move your body at regular intervals and not stay static, to eat healthy organic foods that make your individual body feel good (don't listen to materials written by others that make *them* feel good—how do specific foods make *you* feel?), you *also* make decisions to flip the disease switches to the "off" mode, and the VIBRANT switches to the "on" mode.

Consciously do this, and not only will your overall well-being improve, but so will those of your progeny, for it has been proven that bad habits can be passed down genetically! They may not get into your DNA, but your RNA, which is closely attached to the "map" of your creation. RNA is present in all living cells and is a sort of "messenger" to your DNA.

So pass on the "message" today that you intend to live a healthy life—not just mediocre healthy—but VIBRANTLY healthy and alive and well! MAKE THE DECISION to propel your body to the next level of well-being, where you have an abundance of energy, your immune system is solid, and you don't require as much sleep. That is where *we* are, and it is partially attainable on earth if you learn to transcend the limits of your body by using the willpower of the mind, fueled by the power of your soul's intention to "rocket-evolve" into magnanimous states of ecstasy.

Now doesn't that sound good? *Magnanimous states of ecstasy*. That could be a new book title.

Chapter 6

Flow - Let the Power Run Through You

What happens when you are *not* feeling magnanimous states of ecstasy? Try allowing the POWER to run through you.

What "power" you might ask? The power that creates worlds.

Did you know that there is no such thing as gravity? The earth breathes (expands and contracts) as it faces and turns away from the sun. Your shoes and feet are smaller in the daytime than they are at night. It is scientific fact. It is only the influence of the sun to the speed of a planet.

In the same way, *there is nothing that holds you down.* Everything simply expands and contracts to create a rotation of motion—a centrifugal force—which attracts and repels based on its mass and speed.

Your lungs pump blood to your heart, which pumps blood to the rest of your body. Your body is a miniature "planet," a microcosm of a macrocosmic Universe. We've already pointed out that you are made of the *exact* same properties and materials as the stars and space. And so, why would you *not* harness the power that creates worlds to run through you the way water pours through a faucet?

Regenerate yourself often—perhaps daily or as you gain momentum, in each moment. Just as there is an organic patterning in your biology, there is a cosmic re-patterning happening in your cellular make-up. In other words, *you are evolving in each moment whether you want to or not.*

What this means is that if you are stubbornly refusing to grow, create, learn, and change, you will stay attached to your suffering and inhibit the forward expansion—not just of *you*—but of *all* of us, for once again, *we are all connected.*

Why would you want to do this? Fear? Fear of what? Write it all down now. Go get out your journal. *Please* get it out of your system, for we would like to banish this from our solar system. *Fear does not exist in the dimension where we reside, and it doesn't for you either.* It is *illusion*, based on the transitory state of your body, and the judgment and opinions of others, which do not matter. The more you get in touch and live from your soul's perspective, the less you will feel fear. The less you feel fear, the less you attach to suffering. The less you suffer, the better you will feel. The better you feel, the more goodness you will attract. And finally, the more good you attract—like the centrifugal force of a planet—the more you will be able to give out to "others." For when you give to another, you give to yourself. Expansion, contraction—it's how the planets spin, and it's how you move humanity, by attracting and then giving.

CHAPTER 7

A Leap in Consciousness

So what does it take to make a giant leap in consciousness?

We would say it takes a whole lot of questions. If you've spent your entire life seeking and listening in meditation for the answers to come, then you are quite familiar with this process.

In the asking, a sort of void is created that must be filled. Some religions will tell you that desire is wrong, and yet, desire is part of the growth-seeking mission you signed up for when you came here. It is not the desire that is "wrong," it is simply the thought that you are not already whole as you are.

If you came at the seeking with the belief that you are already whole, the desire would form instantaneously. You may think you believe this, but until it is apparent in the outer material world, this simply isn't so.

And so, we would like you to keep asking questions. Receive the answers from whatever is in front of you—perhaps an overheard conversation, a billboard, nature, a friend, song lyrics. It doesn't matter where the inspiration comes from, as it is your holographic perception bringing it directly to you anyway. You simply must live from a clear mind in order to hear, see, or feel the answers.

What happens when you run out of questions? Here are some more for you:

What makes you feel most alive?

What would make life more meaningful for you?

What is in the way of your peace? What obstacles?

Are you in total peace at this moment? If not, why not?

What would it feel like to live in a state of total peace and serenity? Do you believe that is possible? Why or why not?

Please write down the answers to these somewhere, or sit with them in meditation and watch what comes up. When you've truly answered all of these questions, if more questions do not show up for you (and they might), then you have likely taken a leap of consciousness! As you do this, you connect with the billions of souls who will "feel" your questioning and ask questions of their own.

It is in the seeking that you will find.

Chapter 8

From "Me" to "We" Thinking

You started out as collective souls, part of an all-encompassing field of joy.

You left and returned, left and returned, so as to engage in the thrill of creation and forward-moving expansion. When you left the field of bliss to return to the density of earth, you thought you would remember the field of expansion, but you didn't. You felt it, you unconsciously always knew it was there, but you were too busy creating your own individualized story that you "cut the rope."

The rope is still there. You can find your way home to "we" thinking—of knowing that your soul is joined with another, with all. When you do, when you can find a way to both engage in the creativity and expansion of your individualized mission on earth, as well as connect to the field of bliss that you are always tethered to, you will master the "game" and no longer need to come back. You win.

There is no "fight," for there is no "other." This world is one giant hallucination designed to enable you to win—for us *all* to win. There is no losing because it is a forward-moving Universal field. You begin here by learning what you *don't* want in order to create and appreciate what you *do* want. And then move *beyond* into giving what flows over in your rampant manifestations. That's just where you begin.

To take it a step further—a BIG step—you must not only know and understand that you are part of a giant "WE," not only act like you are part of it by giving generously and often of your gifts and manifestations, but to LIVE from that place and radiate its truth out to humanity.

What would it feel like to live from a place of "we" and not "me"? Would you feel as if you'd lost yourself? Or would you feel as if you were a part of something greater, that you belong in a way that is indescribable, but that you've not felt since you left? When you connect to your "home base," you connect with *bliss*, you connect with everyone and all of us. But when you insist on separating and categorizing yourselves into skin type, genitals, sexual preference, nationality, material belongings, you are just skimming the surface of who you are. Those things are not who you are—you know this by now, don't you?

If you intellectually know this, and you are acting ignorant by judging and condemning and complaining and resisting, you need to go back to the beginning and meditate. Erase all notion of separation by "plugging in" to the greater reality of who you are. You cannot spend time in meditation and still be selfish. It does not work that way. Perhaps selfish is a loaded word. You can be full of "Self," that greater version of you that knows no bounds, and yet, when you realize you are part of the Whole, focusing on the Self is the same as focusing on the All. If instead, you continue plotting about all the items and toys and planetary pleasures you might gain when you focus on attaining them, you will keep coming back until that game wears thin.

You can have *all* you want and more on the other side, in the way station and beyond. You can have all you want and more HERE, if you so desire. The only other step we offer is to give of your time, your talents, and yes, your manifestations. When you clear the attachments to your things and give freely of them, the irony is *they will return to you in boundless form!*

The trick is—and it's not a trick—that you must not intend to give with the notion of it coming back to you. It will, and you must believe it to be so, but do not give only in order to receive. It doesn't work like that. Give and give and give some more, and when it comes back to you, smile at the interplay, and then give again. That's how you win. That's how you gain not just a "happy," life—for happy, like life itself, is transitory. You will instead attain a meaningful life that grows only more and more meaningful as word spreads of its existence. As you radiate the peace and beauty of a life well-lived—full of expansion and giving, faith, abundance, joy, Love, prosperity, health and well-being—you will give others permission to do the same. They don't need your permission, but they still *think* they do. Your example is everything. Your stepping into a BIG, more meaningful and creative life allows for us all to do the same.

Chapter 9

Allergic to Hypocrisy

As you learn to vibrate higher on a consistent basis, you will feel more keenly, and anything that is not the Truth will feel like hypocrisy.

You are in a time of great upheaval. Those who attempt to—as you say—pull the wool over others' eyes in the name of greed will be exposed. You will feel this because big lies are coming to the surface. *You* don't need to expose the Truth—it will be there out in the open as you rise. As you rise, and as you imagine those around you rising up and vibrating at a higher frequency, you will come closer to the space where we are—without bodies—where thoughts are hanging out in the open for all to see.

All thoughts are hanging out in the open right *now*; you just don't choose to see it. Your mind may be still too cluttered by worries and judgments, song lyrics, and desires. When you come from a place where the waters are clear, like a still lake, *that* is when you will know peace. And because you come from a place of peace, you will feel allergic to hypocrisy.

When you are allergic to something, you tend to want to avoid it. For example, Michelle's body is allergic to wheat and dairy. It has negative, painful reactions when she consumes those substances. In the beginning, she would eat them anyway, despite the consequences, until it became too painful to do so.

The same goes for hypocrisy. When you feel as if another is saying one thing and doing another, you will feel the negative polarity in your body first. Don't ignore these feelings! It is not a judgment—it is an avoidance of someone whose lack of authenticity makes you want to gag. Move away. Get out of their vicinity or it will poison you.

Hypocrisy and self-serving greed are at the heart of all conflict. To remedy these ills of your world, what would you say are their opposites? We might say it is living from an open heart, being who you really are and not what others want you to be, and serving the Self by serving others, by giving generously and often.

Is this very hard to do? We think not. When you are in Spirit—and you all will be one day—you will not just live from an open heart, you will BE an open heart. You will know who you really are—LOVE without boundaries or borders. From this space, you will not have the chance to give, for you will have nothing to offer except your Love, which is who you are. Give of yourself now, and you will be one step closer to the higher Truth of who you are, who *we* are, who every single soul is now.

Chapter 10

Holograms

Every single soul is sent here to experience its own holographic reality, projected by its perspective truth, veiled in each situational story line.

What's in yours? Are you experiencing conflict on a personal, cultural, and/or global level?

Is this really a problem with another person, or are you experiencing a reflection of your own inner struggles? Perhaps this could be an opportunity to be freed from old, personal conflicts that are holding you back.

When you start to feel the need to judge, to fight, to resist, please ask yourself what you hope to accomplish? What are you projecting? What are you lending your energy *toward*? What could be the bigger picture of the situation that you might not know in this moment?

We will give, as an example, the situation at Standing Rock in North Dakota. A number of Native American tribes have gathered to protest the laying down of oil pipes through their sacred land and water supply. This began as a peaceful protest, and yet, as many of your peaceful protests do, it has descended into violence. Military forces have been sent out to "control" the situation via force, and veterans joined the cause to protect them.

There have been pledges of money and clothing and shelter to give to those "standing with Standing Rock," and this we see as a good thing, the giving to others. There has currently been a temporary reprieve of the pipeline that the protesters are celebrating, and yet, the incoming administration has promised to privatize those sacred lands, making the situation worse instead of better in the long run. (Update: the new president has signed an executive order to move forward with the pipeline.)

What has happened here? In the "fight" for what's "right," the only thing the Universe "heard"—if the Universe had ears, which it doesn't—is FIGHT. This is a positive, forward-moving expansive cosmos, remember? When you fight anything, it gets bigger and more advanced. There are many others who "prayed" for Standing Rock, and this is doing more than the fighting, you see, for everything starts in the mind. If praying involves asking a deity to come in and save the day, nothing might happen. And yet, if praying involves seeing a peaceful outcome, through visualizations of perhaps everyone having access to clean water, then praying is more active in achieving a peaceful resolution.

We often hear the phrase "just leave it in God's hands." But we would counter that you *are* God's hands. You are in charge of your life; you are the one sending out your own private hologram that soon will not be private anymore. What's in your hologram? Is your mind full of anger and rage, or is it clear and peaceful?

Being angry at others in and of itself is not a bad thing. It is all just energy. Anger may be the impetus for you to channel your energy in a different direction than where it was headed. When you feel angry at another's actions, ask yourself how in any way, shape, or form that anger helps. Feel it, for sure, but then channel it toward the visualization of what it is you *do* want. Move *with* the forward motion of the entire cosmos, not against it. Moving against it will create more resistance, the exact opposite of what you hope to achieve.

In the Standing Rock example, what is the bigger picture? Here we return to self-serving greed. What if you took away your reliance on oil? If you did not consume oil for your cars and engines, you would not have people hurting and killing others in order to make a huge profit from it. Just think of how many people have died in pursuit of a natural resource used for consumption.

How do you "fight" this? You don't. You go back to the drawing board of inspiration and innovation. You create—as you were sent here to do! Create new sources of fuel that aren't limited, and you take the away the power of others to control you.

The holographic story of people "standing off" each other is an old one. It is a hologram of greed triumphing over the powerless, and the powerless gathering in numbers to fight greed. You will not win in this way, you will only battle. You win by creating a new hologram, one where you are self-sufficient and do not rely on the holograms of others. What is in their hologram, do you think? Their hologram is plagued by fears and insecurities, of hatred, bitterness, and vile resentment. Ask yourself: is that what you want in *your* hologram?

Stand together, yes, and visualize a new world, one where people share the bounty they created through a positive, forward-moving momentous hologram, filled with love and peace and joy and bliss. Stand together, yes, but don't stand *against*. That is like a fish swimming upstream, and all that "hard work" that you so prize at this point in time will be for nothing. See the story from where we stand. See the bigger picture; make your own food, clothing, fuel. Go back to basics—then share and give and share some more. Share what you can—more than what you currently *think* you can—for you are a part of an unlimited Universe. See it as that, and it will *be* that. Your hologram is altered by what you feed it with your thoughts and beliefs, and your beliefs are what you obsessively think over and over again. Let go of your addiction to suffering and drama and you will be closer to our reality of peace. Obsessively think of what would make you feel more alive and fulfilled. Be fueled by meaningful activities, and you will flow forward and advance all of humanity.

Focus more on what you *do* want than what you don't want, and then stand together toward *that*.

You see, peaceful protest is an oxymoron. What you want is peace, so gather together for peace. The meaning of protest is to express disapproval or objection to something. Its synonyms include the word "complaint."

Now what do you think happens when you complain on a personal level? You are on a negative frequency channel that only attracts more of the same. Now amplify and multiply those complaints to the level of a protest, and you have an even lower collective vibration. And then you wonder why this low vibration attracts violence.

Although you are not to blame for inciting violence, this is still the result, for it is all about your energetic offering. Standing up is not the same as standing down for a cause. Stand up for peace, but avoid standing off against someone or something.

In the Standing Rock example, if everyone there truly envisioned clean water, they would gain clean water, letting go of exactly how that might occur. But because it seems many others have joined the cause to stand down against what they perceive as the authority, there is more negativity than Light, more "against" than "for," and it remains to be seen what the ultimate result of this clash might be. If there is more praying and chanting than fighting, more gathering in peace than fighting together in numbers, there will be peace. Leave the "protest" out of it and all you have is peace.

Chapter 11

Prisms

We are all prisms of Light, including us.

If your life is like a hologram projecting differing versions of reality based on your thoughts and beliefs and through the lens of your perception, then the Light that comes from your Source Energy—God, Love, whatever you want to call it—is beamed out through the prism that is your body.

If you think of yourself in this way, you'll understand why no two of you are ever alike. When light enters a prism—a sort of geometric pyramid whose end faces are equal and sides are parallelograms—it may refract in millions of different ways. A glass or other transparent object in prism form separates white light into a spectrum of colors.

When you use the word "prism" figuratively, it is in reference to the clarity or distortion created by a particular viewpoint. For example, you might imagine a disaster through the prism of television.

What does this mean? And why are we explaining it to you now?

Any conflicts you might have with another stem from differing versions of reality. Any conflicts one country might have with another country stem from the very same thing. Your cultural belief systems are drawn from centuries of what others have told you, and you swallowed them as your own. They started somewhere in the mind of a man—as in hu-man—and went from thoughts to beliefs to cultural systems to political ideologies and to religious "laws."

But what is *your* Truth?

You see, the only Truth that matters is that, underneath it all, you are made up of Light and Love. Everything else is made-up, an illusion, a trick of the mind. If you were to live in this higher Truth in this moment, and each moment moving forward, you would reside in a state of bliss and peace currently unknown and unrealized. But that is exactly what we are asking you to do right now in order to move humanity exponentially forward. It is that simple.

You might start pointing fingers now and blaming others for your lack of peace—and where does that get you? Right back to conflict and a feeling of unease—and maybe anger and resentment. As a nation, you might collectively point the finger at another nation for the alleged oppression they've waged against you. You might blame your leaders for the laws that separated you and made you feel alone and worthless. But no one can make you feel alone and worthless except for you. Your nationality is a lie. As we've said before, your borders are man-made. Your religions are a way to simplify the Love and Light you already have inside you, a way to contain and control you into believing their thoughts and viewpoints. Your political systems cause the same illusion of derision. All these "systems" are different ways to keep you small, to continue the conflict and drama, to engage in and prolong the suffering.

How do you escape? By opting out. By remembering the true beacon of Light and unconditional Love from which you came, and to which you will return. By reminding each other of who you really are underneath the roles you play in this current lifetime and lifetimes past. By shining as brightly as humanly possible while you are here in your prism, knowing that other prisms are equally beautiful and beam their individual Light spectrum, even when it seems to differ from your own! If all the colors were the same, it would not make such a beautiful rainbow.

Focus on your own rainbow. Perhaps purchase a prism—a crystal—and place it in your window to remind you of who you really are. Watch and observe how the colors change and refract in different hues and at differing angles depending on the time of day and the way that the light enters it. Really stop and observe, and imagine this in your own body, for it is Truth.

CHAPTER 12

The Afterbirth of the New Reality

You are the source of your own pain and your own redemption. You. Not anyone else—for you *are* everyone else.

It is not up to you to wake up the world. That is not your job. Whatever is showing up is pushing you toward more and better.

Michelle has been telling herself a sad story again, one that involves her daughter who is currently not talking to her. This self-imposed darkness is blocking our transmissions. She has been sitting before her computer, wanting, beckoning us to write through her, and she moves deeper into her darkness because she hears nothing.

Have you ever wanted something so badly that you felt angst over not having it? The irony is Michelle has manifested to her heart's desire. She is still playing the game, of course, as this life story of hers is not yet over. But a person is not an object or experience to be attained. Their energy is expressing in a way that only they can truly generate. You are all connected, yes, and yet you all choose to creatively express your very own lifestyles as you see fit.

Ordinarily you manifest by focusing thought on what it is you want, pretending as if you already have it, enjoying the feelings of already having it before it comes into your existence. But if it is a person you "want," whether a lover or a friend or, as in Michelle's case, a relative, they come with their own agenda.

We want you to take a closer look now at that word "relative," which you choose to call your family members.

It means a person connected through blood or marriage, as well as something considered in relation or proportion to something else. Synonyms include: comparative, respective, comparable, correlative, parallel, corresponding.

And so, your "relatives" are all living out their life stories *in relation* to yours. You may compare their corresponding relationships with themselves and others, but it's all inside you. You contain all of their stories—and yet—and this is important: they have not only the right, but the *charge* to move forward in their own parallel Universe, independent from what you want from them.

So what do you do in the meantime?

Rise. Amplify. Ignite. Expand. Repeat.

Start by knowing that the drama is not that person. It is in no way the Truth of their soul's highest path. Kids come into this world with a different agenda than you. Ironically, the more you appreciate the contrast, the less you will need to experience it before skyrocketing out to your manifested desire.

Say to yourself:

"I accept everything as it is, not how I want it to be."

You lack for nothing. It's all a lie.

In trying to rise up yesterday out of her self-imposed "funk," Michelle and Jodah went to see their dream house property. They pretended they were shopping despite not currently seeing the evidence of the money needed to purchase said property. They dutifully walked around neighboring properties that did not quite hold the same "zing" of excitement as the first property they looked at together did! Just like their recent purchase of a mattress, the two of them fell in love with the first mattress they ever laid down on, then did the "right" thing by shopping around other stores for comparable mattresses, before settling on their first love, which came to them easily and effortlessly at a price they could afford.

And so, in the same way, they watched the sun set on their lakefront property. They committed to memory an adjacent property that was in the process of being built from scratch, much in the same way as they hoped to design their home. They ate at a nearby favorite restaurant, pretending it was something they did often, being so close to their new home. And for a little while, Michelle did not worry and fret over her daughter's decision not to talk to her and live out her own self-constructed life story, which did not currently involve Michelle.

This is how you manifest, Dear Ones. Michelle and Jodah will receive the sum for their property from an unexpected source as soon as they can both attain the vibrational frequency to receive it. By practicing the thoughts, feelings, beliefs, and positive expectation that they will indeed live there shortly, it vibrationally has to come. This is not wishful thinking or "hope," it is science. *It's all energy, remember?*

And yet, if Michelle believes she is a bad person because her daughter refuses to talk to her, if she continues to tell herself the sad story that Christmas without her "child," who is no longer a child, would be the saddest, most hurtful thing in the world for her, then she will block the transmission. Those thoughts may come, and she can choose to feel the "sting" of them at first, but it is important she dismiss them as quickly as they come so that she may think a better thought, and feel a better feeling, and climb the road back to Truth, the higher Truth that we are all connected—no matter how it seems—and that her daughter, her *relative*, has the right to live out her own version of things. By living her own best life (that includes her relaxed, lakefront living), she is offering the very best of examples both to her daughter, as well as ALL of her "relations."

Anyone with whom you come in contact is living out their own well-thought out version of life. They decided roughly how this all would interplay before they—before *you*—were even born! In between countless lifetimes, floating around in bliss and joy, they—and YOU—decided to come forth and create, to manifest something from nothing, to remember that you are all connected and therefore have the freedom to act in an appropriate, inspired, loving manner.

Do you remember?

Life is a process of looking forward to things, but doing so lightly. Release your attachment to a "perfect" outcome, for none exists other than advancing humanity forward as a whole.

CHAPTER 13

Feeling Your Soul

Do you need to look at yourself in the mirror to know who you truly are? How does your soul feel?

When you are lying down in the dark, about to go to sleep—when you are in between varying states of consciousness—you may not feel your body.

Stay with us here: if you were to step into a dark room where you had no idea what you looked like, would you still know who you were? If your loved ones stepped into that dark room, would you know who they were despite not using your body senses of sight, smell, hearing, etc.? Could you feel their energy merge with yours but retain your own sense of self?

Sleep sets your soul free when it's not bodily focused. As your body rests, your soul takes off on a journey much like being in what you call heaven, and what we call the way station, for it's a stopover on a way to a much wider and expansive destination.

That is why meditation is so important. That is why the yogis do their stretches prior to final meditation in savasana, or corpse pose—so that their bodies do not hurt and weigh down their souls, and so they might clear their minds in preparation.

You can do this before sleep or just upon waking, or you might do it in meditation. As you gain an awareness outside of the body, your life will improve substantially. We are not saying that your mind is not important, or that your body is not important. You need both your mind and body for this earthly experience. Both are tools, vehicles toward survival. Once you move beyond survival—and we certainly hope you have if you've read all our books up until now—you move closer to the soul's guidance. It is there you will find freedom from suffering. It is there where you will find certain bliss—again, not happiness, for happiness is a transitive state based on pain or pleasure.

Bliss has no standards, it just is.

Chapter 14

Encoding vs. Decoding

See the symbolism in your life's program. You were the developer who encoded it into your system before you were born.

Do you remember?

Everything in nature repeats itself as patterns, and so does your existence. Look for the themes, the clues you left so you might remember your higher Truths. **Decode your life.**

Do you know that the meaning of "cosmos" is the Universe seen as a well-ordered whole; *and second,* as a system of thought.

There is a reason for which you gave this word this meaning. The entire cosmos is inside of *you*. There is no higher power than the one that gives you strength! When you surrender to your higher power, please do not interpret this as giving away your power and doing nothing. When you surrender to your higher power, you are allowing your system of thought to merge with the entire forces of the Universe, seen as a well-ordered whole. That is the true meaning of becoming "whole."

When you sleep, when you rest, when you are present in nature—and yes, when you meditate—you become one with the cosmos. As you do so, you will be more present to your entire life. And when there are "glitches," you will catch them instantly and reroute the perceived problem. You will see the overarching themes governing your story, and you will align with their highest purpose and remember to find compassion and love within each situation. You will get stronger, yes, not physically but spiritually—in the sense that you are Spirit—and you remember this in each moment.

When you identify more with your bodily self than your soul self, you will suffer pain and hardships. *When you are more addicted to your hardships than to your peace, you will create suffering for those around you.* This is currently happening everywhere in your world. And yet, if you get addicted to the world's suffering more than your own peace, you will never find a way or the will to transcend it all. It is an illusion, remember? A sort of computer program you developed from your soul to find joy. The "others" who are not *others* but all a part of You, also are playing the game. Your interference, once more, is not asked for or welcomed. Feel compassion, yes, feel unconditional love toward all the players, and transcend the suffering, knowing how unreal it truly is. Assist in manifesting the survival needs for all, so they can be in the game they chose. Beyond that, it's their game, their story. They—and you—will all "die" in the end, that is a given. You know the ending of your story already—you do not need to read ahead.

And what we are here to tell you is that your "life" goes on far beyond the game, the story. From your physical experience, you cannot understand this. And yet, as you have more and more extended moments of transcending the body, you will know and realize this Truth that we may only point to with your words. Death is only of the body. You get do-overs to repeat varying storylines that mimic your movies and television scripts. But you don't have to do it over and over again. *Why do it the hard way?*

CHAPTER 15

The Easy Way

*T**he easy way is to know peace and to amplify that peace.* The easy way is to rest more and do less, to take action only when inspired to do so from a place of peace and serenity. The easy way is to move around your world and observe the beauty of it. Witness the beauty and leave behind the judgment and comparisons of "other" cultures and traditions, for they are just various and diverse expressions of creativity.

Make a list of ways in which people are the same versus different. Have your children do this while they are still young and don't "see" the differences you might. Your same list is longer. You are more the same than you believe, and you might appreciate more the way you choose to create and explore this level of reality.

Hear this: even violence is creative expression. You will hate hearing this, and yet it is true. *Violence is simply a primitive way of expressing negative emotions.* When you have negated all such emotions—of frustration and resentment and anger and fear—your world will know peace. And yet, when you meditate you will often find these feelings surface from within you. Do not be afraid of them, for they are a gift!

See them, feel them, embrace them, release. Repeat this process as often as necessary, as if you were doing the laundry, and with that level of unconcern.

You have all experienced violent lifetimes in which you were the bad guy in the story. There is no need to forgive yourself for this, or to wring your hands in guilt and sorrow. It was a role in a play you chose to evolve your soul and advance humanity—and the entire cosmos—forward. That's all it is. And when others seem to hurt you or hurt those you love, remember that it is indeed a story. It sure won't feel like it, but if you can feel first and then transcend your vengeful feelings, you will help your world in a very big way.

At any given time you may say aloud that you will use your will to change the plot. You can do this through a strongly held intention, backed with the realization that you don't need to suffer unnecessarily. Take ownership of any energy you are sending out that may attract the vibration of violence, and simply change direction. Choose a path of trust and faith and flowing *with* the cosmos, not against it, and you will rise above the frequency of fear and violence. Remember, both are of the body. You can't have fear without a body, and you can't perform or receive an act of violence unless you have a physical body. You only do that stuff here. Do you find it interesting that you often use the phrase an "act" of violence? Also, that someone "performs" an act of violence. Both are *acting* terms, yes? Further evidence that at some level you all must know that this life is all a stage, just as Shakespeare wrote so long ago.

"All the world's a stage, And all the men and women merely players; They have their exits and their entrances, And one man in his time plays many parts, His acts being seven ages." ~from *As You Like It*.

Chapter 16

Hope is a Powerful Emotion

On the "scale" of emotions, when you reach the register of "hope"—when you attain the frequency of it, or at least get in the same ballpark—you are on your way to achieving a new level of peace, understanding, and positive expectation.

What is before hope on the scale? Leading up to it are fear, despair, hatred, resentment, and anger. But once you attain hope, the scale tips toward appreciation, gratitude, love, joy, and bliss. Hope is the pivoting point. When you are down, hope is the level you want to reach.

Michelle and Jodah had a teacher once who said that hope was a "negative" word, that it was passive in attaining your desires. And in that respect, it could be interpreted as such; for example, "I sure hope I get that job." A more powerful affirmation might be: "I now have a job that I love, that I wake up to eagerly each morning and get excited about showing up to. In fact, it's so fun that it doesn't feel like 'work,' and I get so in the flow that time seems to stand still. My job is in a beautiful environment, and I'm surrounded by beautiful, supportive people who all enjoy this job as much as I do! I receive money from this as well as other unexpected sources of income, and all my debts are paid easily and effortlessly, with an abundance of surplus to share!"

Okay, well that would be the long version, but you get the idea. You can word this in your own way, but the key is to feel the emotions of hope and positive expectancy while you are stating the words and imagining them happening in reality. Start with hope, and from there it becomes an easy climb to the top. In fact, it doesn't feel like a "climb" at all—more like a downhill ride on a bicycle as any resistance disappears!

Yesterday, Jodah discovered his job of many decades might very well disappear in a few weeks. He had wanted to leave this job for quite some time, and actively using the tools we have shown him to manifest more fulfilling work that met his new higher level of understanding and growth. And yet, he had obstacles in the past that made him feel that if he left this work he would be letting his coworkers down. And so, the manifestation became that the entire company was "let go" so that no one person would be let down.

Do you see what a beautiful example of vibrations this is?! His only "job" now is to maintain the highest frequency he can hold consistently while clarifying what his new path is. If he can stay out of fear and the lower vibing emotions, and stay in a space of trust and faith and openness to new adventures and opportunities, this is the very thing he wanted to create!

As for the "others," they are all HIM. You are all each other, remember? There is only and ever ONE Spirit flowing through all souls. Each soul will find its new path toward greatness, or will succumb to fear and self-loathing and go deeper down as so many of you humans are prone to do.

We want you to stop this. We want you to see things from our bigger and broader perspective, from the eyes of your greater Spiritual being rather than the limited vision of your smaller egoic self who strives to make everything about its *one* self rather than a gift for all mankind.

Staying in your power is a gift to humanity, not just to yourself. When faced with something "scary," we want you to remember that without a body, there is no fear. If you were to lose your job and your home and had no food, and therefore perished, that is the worst possible thing that could happen to you—and yet, it wouldn't really, would it? When you die, as we have explained, you go "home" to the most beautiful unconditionally loving and light-filled experience you could possibly ever imagine! Hopefully, one of your brethren will come along to help you with your basic survival needs, as that is what we are encouraging all of you to do for each other in the name of enjoying a peaceful co-existence, with abundance and plenty for all.

When Jodah heard news about the potential ending of his career, Michelle was in a different space entirely. She had traveled outside of her house to a nearby coffee shop that she loved, and she was going over the edits for the last book we wrote together. She was distracted by the beauty of the courtyard, and she was already in a state of hopefulness that things always work out in her favor.

The day prior, a nurse called Michelle to follow up on her stem cell treatment from nine months ago. Michelle has been diagnosed with an autoimmune disease, and the treatment promised to re-grow the digestive tissues that were decimated by her body's attack against itself. We will get into the meaning of autoimmune in a moment—please stay with us...

Michelle revealed that she had not felt any progress with the treatment, and she still experienced extreme intermittent stomach pain. The nurse told her that the amniotic fluid cells that were injected into her body would be reproducing for at least another three months, and potentially the next three years! Michelle asked about the nurse practitioner who had injected her with the treatment. Had her symptoms alleviated? As it happened, that nurse practitioner synchronistically shared the same Celiac disease as Michelle and was receiving the treatment the same day—talk about sharing the same exact frequency!

After speaking with the nurse practitioner, the nurse called Michelle back to tell her that said nurse practitioner had been completely healed.

Michelle now had hope that she too could be healed. And as we've said, hope is a powerful emotion.

So what is an autoimmune disease?

Your body's ingenious immune system was designed by you to attack foreign invaders that cause infection. But when your immune system overreacts, it targets its own body tissues.

This is very important for you to understand in a larger context, so please pay attention.

When you are in a state of fear—not momentarily, because that is going to happen from time to time in a human lifetime experience and is designed to get you out of trouble fast—but when you *remain* in a state of fear over long periods of time, your cells feel the unrest and attack anything and everything. Your fearful vibration sends messages throughout your body to attack and kill, not differentiating between what is truly an attack and what might be healthy cellular growth for your body's overall health and well-being.

In the same way, when you are in a chronic state of fear, you might physically or emotionally attack everything and anyone in your path, even yourself! And when entire communities do this, when entire nations remain in a heightened state of fear and alienation, they vibrate on the frequencies of violence and war. That is how bad decisions are made, out of extreme and long-standing states of fear.

How you "undo" this hyper-fearful state of attack mode is simply to alleviate it in yourself, for again, you are all connected. What you heal in yourself you heal in your holographic world reality! When are you going to truly believe us on this one? It's the main reason you don't currently live in a blissful state of peace—you have not conquered it in yourself.

It is said there are more than 80 types of autoimmune diseases, and no one knows for sure what causes them. They cause inflammation and swelling, as well as a whole lot of pain and suffering.

We know exactly what causes these diseases—*dis*-ease; the opposite of ease, which is fear. Flip switch it to "hope" and you will cure yourself. Cure yourself, and you cure all of humanity.

Don't have an autoimmune disease? We beg to differ. You all experience bodily inflammation; it just doesn't show up in the same way for everyone. But we promise you, if in the very moment you receive "bad news" you realize it just isn't real, that things are always working out for you, that you live and engage in a positive, forward-flowing Universe of expansion, then you will instantaneously live in perfect health and freedom!

As an infant, you knew this. Right out of the way station, you still had one foot on the earth and one foot in the realm of pure peace and bliss and total understanding. When you are about to die, you will realize this again, for you are stepping one foot onto the other side and into the next dimension. That's why so many of you see those who have passed before you greet you and assist your transformation.

Alleviation of fear is true freedom. When you die, you experience the higher Truth of your being, which is pure peace and freedom. When you can talk yourself out of fear, you are talking your world out of fear and attachment to suffering. When you move from despair to hope, from hope to gratitude, and from gratitude to joy, you lead by example and others will feel the strength of your path and rejoice.

We have told Michelle to believe in our books, and that when she does, so will the "others." And when Jodah believes in limitless expansion, as they wish to call their future workshops with us, he will continue to grow and expand, and not through fear and suffering, but through hope and trust and faith. If they can do it, so can you.

You are all connected.

You are all connected.

You are all connected.

Chapter 17

Which Future do You Want to See?

Let's say you are at what you call a "crossroads" situation. You are faced with something big that will alter the course of your life. *What do you do?*

Instead, ask the question: "How will I *feel*?" How you feel sets the course of your new reality. How you choose to feel is the tuning fork for the vibrational channel of the "you" that you wish to tap into, the dimensional self that plays out accordingly.

Let's give you an example. As we mentioned before (with their permission), Jodah and Michelle are facing Jodah's job loss because of his company's restructuring. They could either prepare for the worst or plan for the best. Either way they will be okay. But in one scenario they are worrying and fretting and anticipating how their lifestyle will get worse while they imagine a life of lack. And in a different scenario, they are still looking ahead and paving the way for a lifestyle filled with all the things they might enjoy and derive pleasure from: a lakefront house, plenty of travel, high-vibing friends, and ever-flowing income from a variety of expected and unexpected sources.

In another example, Michelle's friend—we will call her Susan—just discovered she is pregnant with her second child. She had wanted to be pregnant, and so this is joyful news! And yet, her first child is an adult and she is in her mid-40s. There are many statistics about women having babies as they get older, and none are positive. Those statistics say that she should never have gotten pregnant in the first place! She had a .06% shot of conceiving, yet that baby soul has already beaten the odds! Now her doctors are warning her with all kinds of bad news, but she is not listening. She is focusing on the fact that she is healthier now than she was in her 20s. She is focusing on the image of a happy, healthy, full-term baby that will bring her and her fiancé great joy. As long as she can keep her "channel" tuned into positive images and aspects, she will enjoy a happy, meaningful, positive family life.

It is in the times of our greatest fear that we have the power to turn things around by changing the channel and tuning into a more positive experience. It's time you use this power to its full extent—not just for your personal pleasure, but to affect the humanity of your human race for good! There are some who say when injustice becomes law, resistance becomes duty. We say the opposite is true if you want peace. Resistance creates more resistance, which FEEDS injustice! You can stop the flow of fear by changing the channel to one of faith. Suffering is no longer essential to your survival; you just don't see proof of it yet.

Michelle was scrolling through social media the other day when she saw a video of a man in Aleppo, Syria, pleading for his life. That region is war torn and everyone seems to be fighting over it. The victims caught in the crossfire are not able to receive any aide. Michelle perceived it as a very sad situation, and she was filled with empathy.

Michelle wanted to DO something about this. She began to become enraged at their plight because it seemed hopeless and she felt powerless to change it. You might feel this way also, perhaps not about the situation in Syria, but about the many perceived injustices and grave situations in your world.

That is the world of pain and violence. Remember, that is not your world any longer. You can no more change anyone else's path than you can change the flow of the oceans. Just as you have learned your lessons from contrast, the whole WORLD is learning its lessons from contrast. It is not your job to interfere. You may have compassion for them, knowing their inner soul shares the same Spirit as you. You may do your best to give generously so that they may be fed and sheltered and protected as much as possible. If you are in a position of power, you may do your best to lead by example, with honesty and integrity.

But if you are not in a leadership position, your being angry about the situation will only bring you more pain and suffering, and this energy will only lend itself to all the anger and pain and suffering in the situation itself.

When you begin to feel the pangs of powerlessness, please stop yourself and wish them joy. Imagine healing light pouring throughout the region, filling their rivers and streams and oceans. Imagine those faces you see in the news, the faces of pain and anguish and suffering, filled with light and laughter and love! Picture them laughing, for you cannot be addicted to your suffering when you are laughing. Go ahead, please do it now. Spend some time with this, visualizing Light and Love and peace and joy. Lend that Light to your friends and neighbors.

This is NOT a passive activity! This is the way to peace. Don't ever think for a moment that your energy is not a powerful force for good. It is the most powerful force there is, for it flows with the tide of the entire Universe behind it.

Perhaps try this now with a "smaller" personal situation. Shed some light on it. Picture the person(s) involved surrounded in flowing light. Maybe give that light a color. What color is the light you are visualizing? Don't overthink this—the first color that comes to mind is the best.

Michelle has been visualizing pink light flowing through her daughters, both of them. They are both going through various difficult lessons, and as she does not wish to alter the course of their life's direction and lessons—even if they are harsh ones—she wants them to feel both her love and the greater Love of who they truly are. As she has been doing this more often, she has sat back and watched miracles play out! Her children are private people, and so she has asked us not to give examples here, but suffice it to say they are not just surviving, but thriving! And isn't that what we all want for our children?

That kind of love and peace can travel all over your world if you really want it to. It takes dedication to flip-switch your outrage to one of peace every single time it surfaces, but in time, it will evolve to a natural gut reaction, one where you will not have to think before you launch into your loving light meditation.

Chapter 18

How are You Praying?

Have you been praying for something to manifest or change, and yet sat by hopelessly while nothing seemed to happen?

The answers may lie in *how* you've been praying and the energy you've expressed.

The modern definition of prayer is a solemn request for help or expression of thanks addressed to God or an object of worship.

An example of this is: "I'll say a prayer for him."

We would like to ask you to honestly think about whether you actually take time to visualize this person in peace and good health when you say that you'll say a prayer for them, or if you are just saying this because you feel sorry for them and wish to do something, or express your empathy?

Another definition of prayer is: an earnest hope or wish.

And so, if you are earnestly hoping that someone's situation changes for the better, in harmony with the natural forward-moving, ever-changing progress of the entire Universe, then we want you to actually take a moment (or several) to envision a positive outcome for more dramatic results.

The action of visualizing another bathed in Light and Love does not go against their soul's agreement or purpose—it can't. If you envision an outcome for someone that is something YOU want, not something they may want—even if it's destructive and may do them harm—that is a wish from ego. *Sometimes what is best and fastest for a soul's growth is still learning through suffering.*

But visualizing a person or a situation bathed in Light and unconditional Love is simply seeing them for the Truth of who they are beneath their skin and the various roles they play in life. Holding space for that, seeing the Truth of who they are, and the Light you share, will do more for them than if you say in passing that you will pray for them and do nothing, expecting a deity to do the work for you.

You see, the word "prayer" is based on the Latin word "precarius" which translates into "obtained by entreaty." The definition of "entreaty": an earnest or humble request.

In and of itself, this word is a harmless emission of surrender and hope, but it is only a starting point, you see.

The modern definition of "precarious" means: not securely held or in position; dangerously likely to fall or collapse; or dependent on chance; uncertain.

Of course, the word is also from the original Latin word "precarius," the same exact origin of "prayer"—meaning "obtained by entreaty."

What does this mean for you?

You've been praying all wrong! That's why you haven't received the consistent results you desire. If prayer, as you know it, is uncertain or likely to fail, and dependent on chance, how dependable is it?

If your belief in a deity more powerful than you is keeping you from being the powerhouse of Light that you truly are, you need to rethink your belief systems. Is this belief in a higher power outside of yourself helping or hurting you and your "brethren"—the others who share your Spirit, your Light? Remember, beliefs are simply thoughts you think over and over again. Who gave you those thoughts to begin with?

Was it your parents, your teachers, your society, your religion? What is it that *you* really believe in? Do you believe in *You*? CAN you believe in YOU as an extension of Spirit, translated as a soul moving forward?

A better way to go about it is to wake each morning renewed and refreshed, happy to be alive, grateful for all you have. A better way to go about it is to see a shining, bright Light raining down health, wealth, wisdom, love, and all manner of abundance upon all your friends and family first, and then extending this light-filled vision toward the world. Perhaps focus the Light (not your Light, for you are not giving away your own Light, you are LENDING it to join with everyone in your path) on a situation that is displeasing to you—perhaps an illness or injury, a perceived situation of "lack"—financial or otherwise. Perhaps you long for your soul mate, and he or she has not materialized yet. You will do more to manifest this person in your life by shining Light upon yourself than you will to endlessly date or worse, stay home and feel bad about yourself. You are never, ever alone. You are one Light of many. Rain Light and Love on yourself each day, and you will attract a higher vibing partner who both sees and amplifies your Light and growth. As you grow and develop, share and shine your Light on others. As you learn to "lend" your Light, you will see situations change as if miraculously! Your income will increase, your health and well-being will be lit up, your relationships will all improve…what else could you possibly want on this planet?

Oh yes, back to the subject of this book: peace and plenty and propulsion. When you are lending your Light, you *must* be at peace. There is no other way. Please read that again. As you lend your Light often and well, you will not only affect your personal situations, but that of the entire world. When you are at peace more often than you are stressed and in strife, you see the holographic reality of your world changed and affected by your vision. And as you do this, you will live in a world of plenty—not just for those at the top of the food chain, but for you and ALL souls, living and dead, human and animal. This is the heaven you asked for, the "entreaty" you've been putting out there. Claim it now by seeing the Light and lending it out to many to create a beacon of hope and joy.

As Michelle wrote this and practiced it, she witnessed what she still deems "miracles" in her life stories. They are not "miracles" if they happen often, for they are no longer what you call extraordinary, they are daily reality. Jodah's precarious job situation as an independent contractor changed to a steady job as an employee—with a slight raise in income! He longs to change this line of employment within the year, and his frequency brought this situation to the forefront, you see. Jodah is now more motivated to experience the change to a life of freedom and purpose, not an existence changed to someone's whim. We find it amusing that so many of you call your job a "stable" salary when it is anything but. Nothing is stable. *Nothing*. Everything is moving and changing constantly in the Universe, as is Jodah. When Michelle shined her Light upon the situation, it gave them a reprieve, a baby step forward as they continue to work on our creative projects and watch them blossom and thrive.

Michelle also shined more Light on her situation with her teenage daughter, who agreed to go to mediation with her this week, right before Christmas! (Update: they have made peace in their relationship!)

During these "trials," Michelle and Jodah continued reminding themselves that things are always working out for them, and so it is. There is no true "trial," except in your own minds. Shine the Light, let it go. Know that this is the most active, powerful act you can harness! Going out and fighting someone lends to the fight, to the resistance. When you fight the power, you add power to the fight. But going within and envisioning the energy of Love and Light, and lending it to your neighbors throughout the world, will propel you forward faster than you ever thought possible.

Chapter 19

We are Not the Only Ones

We want you to contemplate something for a moment. There are currently 7 billion people on your planet. In the past, there have been fewer bodies inhabiting Earth at any given time. And yet, what this means is that people are dying all the time. And also rebirthing back to life, but mostly dying. As they give their bodies back to the earth, their spirits take flight and go "home," back to the way station and beyond into new dimensions. There are more spirit-souls than earthly bodies, yes? You understand the math?

Some of these souls go right back into the game, rejoining the familiar path of a life learned through suffering and growth. Others tire of the game, and float in bliss without a body to drag them down. Still others rise higher and come together to teach peace and wisdom. Such is our mission.

We are simply not the only ones. There are a *whole* lot of divine teacher-spirits who might guide you, and yet too often you are so mindful and focused on your supposed trials and tribulations that you ignore and block us.

The other day, Michelle's computer was not working. It told her it was "not responding" and frustrated her because she could not work on our book. When Michelle is "not responding," our words—and other divine guidance—cannot flow through. The results showed up in her body as a migraine and constipation. The answer was to stop everything and partake in abundant self care. In Michelle's case, this was a mani/pedi for her fingers, toes, and soul. When she was finished, she felt renewed, and the aforementioned breakthroughs happened for her and those she loved! Later, her friend Amy gave her an energy healing, clearing even more "residue" accumulated from taking on other people's problems. She really needs to stop doing that.

Chapter 20

G.O.D. = Goodness Oriented Direction

When you feel blocked, you can indeed ask for Divine assistance.

We have never said that there is no such thing as God. We would just like to point out here how primitive it is to believe that your God looks exactly like you do. We know that the Bible says that God made himself in the form of man, but do you always believe everything you read? That book was written more than two thousand years ago. From today's perspective, and all that you have learned in the past few centuries, does it seem plausible that a man (with skin and genitals) lives in the sky and judges and directs your every move? It's not likely.

You would do well to envision your God as an acronym for "Goodness Oriented Direction." In this image, you are the vessel, and God is more like the wind in your sails, helping you move forward with the natural movement of the entire Universe. In this image, *you* are the one with the power. YOU are the one who created form from thought between lifetimes, and continue to do so now, albeit a little more slowly now that you are in a denser form. *You* did this, not some man in the sky. If there were indeed a man in the sky, he would not be able to breathe oxygen as you do here on the planet, you see? "He" is gender neutral, as there is no body, just as when you return to your spiritual self as a soul you no longer inhabit a body.

If you can learn to harness the power of this version of "God," you will surrender to a much more powerful "wind beneath your wings." You will not have to "do" anything other than listen for intuitive guidance and follow through with inspired action to create the heaven on earth that, through the centuries (going back to biblical days), you've always said you wanted.

Be smarter with this. Believe in a force greater than your *self* with a lowercase "s." Believe your soul is part of something much more expansive, a force that is one with God as a goodness oriented direction, and you will enjoy a grand life, full of grace and flow and abundance of every kind.

Believing in this version of God as forward-moving flowing expansiveness in a positive direction will propel your people exponentially, as *we* have always wanted for you. This is why we are here, you see. We want to see you evolve more rapidly, and this is a big part of the "how" you can do it together.

So don't preach. When asked about God, you can say you believe that God is a goodness oriented direction, and that believing that way makes you feel amazing. Because you believe in God as a universal force for goodness, magical things happen, and your only wish is to share the good things you manifest for one another to create a more peaceful, plentiful existence for everyone. How can "they" argue with that?

Well, they can argue, because so many of you are set in your ancient belief systems that are based on thoughts that were once fed to you, and that you now obsess over. Stopping that momentum of thousands of years may take some time, but time doesn't exist, remember? And so, take all the "time" you need. Live from a place of God as expansiveness and growth, and watch how your life's bounty increases. Give from that surplus, and allow others to watch your example. Some will tag along, inspired by your vision, and others will continue to believe in a punishing, angry God-person and their world will reflect that image.

Chapter 21

Don't Change the Channel

When you *do* begin to live with the wind beneath your wings, and you *do* ask for greater guidance and receive it daily, you will glow from within. As you radiate, there will be those who try to emulate you. And still, there will be those who will vehemently oppose the "new" you that is, in fact, the old you—the very, very old soul beneath the superficial role you've been playing out through your ego personality and the storyline you chose this lifetime around.

You know what happens when you make a big change—or any change for that matter? You say that not only do you have a tough time initiating it (not true, as you are always changing and growing, and your resistance makes you ill), but when you *do* find the courage to go with your heart's desire—as you were intended to do—it intimidates those who stubbornly choose not to.

Those others in your midst who do not appreciate the glowing new/old you who radiates goodness (in the natural order of things, as we pointed out in the last chapter) will try to convince you to be where *they* are. They, in fact, might be completely ill—in body or emotion—and yet, they will staunchly hold their position that "familiar" is best. Or even worse, they might suggest that miserable is best. But by now, you surely know better.

The better you feel, the better you will feel. And the better you feel, the more you will attract the good into your life. The more good you attract, the more you will be able to give to others and have it return to you tenfold. That's how this whole thing works.

For some who are watching you, they will be elated as you share with them both your joy and your bounty. And still others will want to change you back or for the worse.

Know that no one can take down your vibe but you. When you are strong in your frequency, being in the midst of a low-vibe person can only make you stronger. If you succumb to their lower vibe, it is because you are still wavering. There may be a part of you that "feels badly" for them. And yet, it is their personal choice to feel bad, not yours.

Imagine you are in your car with a passenger, and your passenger doesn't like the radio station. Unless one of you reaches out and pushes a button or turns the dial, nothing will change. The same is true for your own frequency channel. Unless you decide to change it, no one else can. It's your "car." You are in the driver's seat.

If other people—"relatives" as we described earlier, relative to your frequency—try to "take you down," simply don't let them. Ignore their name calling, their childish behavior, their temper tantrums, and go do something enjoyable for yourself that will either lift—or at the minimum—maintain your frequency. Listen to music, walk in nature, take a bath, do some yoga or other form of meditation—by now you have your own personalized list of "feel good" action items, yes?

If you do not, or if you feel as if that list is evolving, make a new one! This should be a fun activity based on your latest vibrational offering, which is ever changing. Just because you enjoyed dancing last year, it doesn't mean you won't like hiking more this year. If you find yourself saying you don't like an activity, perhaps take the "don't" out of your vocabulary and retry the activity to see if you've changed your mind.

You are always entitled to change your mind! In fact, if you are not changing your mind often and daily, we would say you are stuck, and you are always asking us why you are "stuck."

That is what you might call "getting in your own way"—deciding you don't like something or someone based on past experience. What is your experience right now, in this present moment? You might not even know yet, so try it again please. Life is supposed to be full of many enjoyable things and pleasures, people and activities, and adventures. Try them all *now* so that they will fill your memory banks with pleasure in the afterlife, in the way station, and beyond. *There are no regrets in other dimensions, only in your current lifetime.* So get out there and make some changes, and don't listen to those who might tear you down. That is their evolutionary path to take, and it is a slower and more arduous one.

Chapter 22

All This is Happening So That You May Find Peace

Whatever it is you are facing is helping you learn inner peace. We have said in the past that there are no problems in Truth. You are still learning lessons, but you don't have to suffer over them if you understand they are always—and unequivocally—about finding your peace, speaking your peace, knowing your peace, living out your peace.

Let's be clear about this: peace is always ever and only the lesson. In fact, it is the only lesson you need ever learn.

We will give as an example Michelle and Jodah's current situations. Michelle found a mediation center to resolve the perceived differences between her and her teenage daughter, and her daughter agreed to go. Two mediators heard varying sides of their stories for a full three hours, inserting questions here and there for clarity. There were lots of tears. Michelle cried all the way home because she didn't feel heard at all; she felt blamed and judged and misunderstood. We cannot speak for how her daughter felt, but she refused to spend Christmas with Michelle, which hurt her deeply—emotionally, that is.

Let's break this down for her and for you all as well, for we are sure that you have faced similar perceived struggles as you "bump" up against one another's viewpoints. Michelle sees herself in a certain way, in a certain "light," as you say. Her daughter is at an age where she wishes to differentiate herself from her mother, and so she is pointing out all of her mother's faults and mistakes in order to separate.

If Michelle could have risen above and seen the big picture of what was happening, she would not have taken this so personally. Instead, she felt attacked—sad, angry, hurt, resentful. All of those lower vibrational emotions triggered memories that have a similar vibrational component in her past, and thus began a downward spiral into depression.

She curled up in a ball in her bed for a few days with zero energy because she allowed herself to be drained emotionally. Michelle's elder daughter came to visit for the holidays, which was a definite improvement. But still, as they opened presents on Christmas morning, as is your ritual, she felt her youngest daughter's absence and cried some more.

In Jodah's situation, as we mentioned, he was faced with the loss of his long-time job. He no longer enjoys this job and has been longing for a different way to earn income that is rewarding and pleasurable and serves humanity better. Do you relate to this perhaps?

Then he learned that his job was spared. He "should" have felt grateful, but instead he felt let down. He still had to go back to the job he dislikes. His body rebelled; his shoulder and neck have been in a great deal of physical pain from spending long hours at his desk, combined with resenting the work he's doing.

Now, he still has a form of income to live the lifestyle Michelle and Jodah currently enjoy. And yet, Jodah has been, in effect, physically and emotionally paralyzed from completing projects he simply doesn't want to do.

So what are they to do? It is not often that the two of them are in a funk at the same time, but of course we understand it from an energetic perspective, yes? They are simply on the same "wavelength," as you say. It's just not a good one to be on.

Michelle suggested they "change the channel" by going into their hot tub, for starters. While in the soothing hot water, they discussed all the things they were grateful for—and there was *a lot*! They spoke of their plans for us—The Power of 10—and how they were going to market and edit our books and travel and spread our messages in the New Year. And then, they laughed at the concept of a brighter new year, as so many of you look to, because it is all man-made, you see. You don't need a calendar to start over. Each moment is an opportunity to do so!

Of course, we support the energetic offering that the promise of a new year, and a new "you," brings. We would just like to add that you can do that in December as well as in January—or in April for that matter.

We are going off topic. As Michelle and Jodah began to speak of newer, brighter things than their current perceived obstacles to their ultimate happiness, they began to smile and laugh again. They got out of the hot tub, and Michelle massaged Jodah's back, neck, and shoulders (Michelle is a former certified massage therapist—so this should be a no-brainer, as you say). As Michelle was fully present in order to assist Jodah's healing, she wasn't thinking and obsessing and focusing on her impasse with her daughter. When she finished, her daughter texted her and thanked her for her thoughtful Christmas presents. She also told her that she loved her.

You see, things are never as bad as they seem, and you are closer energetically at any given time than you may perceive. You all want pleasure and to avoid pain. You all want human connection, and the irony is that at any given time you are all already connected spiritually!

So the energetic spiraling changed its course for both Michelle and Jodah, and they spent the rest of the evening researching the Caribbean island of Curacao for their next trip, and potentially as a place to work and reside. As they both studied the advantages of this beautiful island, they grew more hopeful and excited. As they grew more excited, their energetic offering lifted. As their energetic offering lifted, they changed the channel to a more positive station. Jodah is still sleeping as Michelle writes these words, so it remains to be seen if he can maintain this new and improved "wavelength." But if he can, he doesn't need to "figure out" a thing. All will be drawn to him—from new sources of income, to opportunities, to travel adventures, to friends and other like-minded individuals who might show him new avenues for growth. (Update: Michelle was offered an opportunity to speak on a cruise to Curacao the very next day!)

This is how you do it, folks. You don't have to have the same perceived "problems" as the examples we just laid out for you. And this is not a "problem" competition. You may see your obstacles as far worse than the ones Jodah and Michelle are currently facing, or yours might seem comically easier by comparison. IT DOESN'T MATTER! You lift your vibration in the same way—by doing the things you enjoy, talking more about the things you love than the things you dislike, and dreaming and visualizing creative ways to improve your current situation and surroundings. That's it. Let everyone do it in their own way. Instead of getting into the hot tub, it may be a nice long walk that gets the process started. It may be calling a friend, or grabbing a cup of coffee, or writing a poem. It could be that all you have energy for is diverting your mind with an uplifting movie or book, or flipping through a magazine for ideas. You know YOU best. Stop dwelling on the perceived problem for a while, and watch how your lack of focus on it makes it fade away.

Chapter 23

The Universe does not Create Your Authenticity—You Do

By becoming "real," you tap into universal forces that are unstoppable. When you become someone else (i.e., pretend to take on a different role than the one in your heart), you lack purpose, and you run around asking, "What's my purpose?" over and over again.

The answer is right in front of you! We have told you again and again that your only true purpose is to love. When you die, when you return to the space between lifetimes that we like to call the "way station" and you often call "heaven," you are nothing *but* Love. "Love is all there is," as you sing in your songs.

And so, a question you might ask instead is, "How am I NOT showing love?" That will reveal your perceived "block," and it usually involves not being authentically yourself.

When you were a small child, you did not pretend to be anyone other than yourself. Sure, you had imaginary play, but that is not what we are talking about here. When you were hungry, you cried for food.

When your diaper was wet, you cried to have it changed. When you developed words, you asked for things without pretense. Later, you learned to manipulate by observing the people in your midst and their interactions with you and each other. Much later, in your adolescent years, you became self-conscious and lost self-worth—or you developed an over-inflated ego based on lost self-worth. Either way, your true self-worth was hidden as you tried on the various roles that others laid out before you—whether it was your well-intentioned parents or your manipulative parents (as the case might be), or societal rules or norms, or friends or even your own children—you became someone you are *not* in order to please someone else, yes? You may have even done this to prove to yourself you are worthy, which, of course, you've already been since birth (and, we might add, throughout eternity).

You are always worthy, no matter what role you play. So you might as well play one that works for you and brings you joy!

How are you *not* showing your love? Where do you hold back? If you are still using money as the reason you are not doing what you love to do—that which lights you up and serves humanity and feels natural and light—you need to go back and reread our first two books.

What does being fully YOU look like? When Michelle revealed her full intuitive abilities, there were some who mocked her and called her a "fake"—ironically, for being fully real and herself. And surprisingly (to her), many more who believed in her and felt gratitude for her innate gifts that she used—and continues to use by being the vehicle for our messages—to help others grow and develop and evolve.

Michelle has friends who are homosexual and who had to hide a big portion of who they really were throughout most of their lives because of possible fallout and rejection. Some have even had to fear for their lives in parts of your world! And yet, when the pain of not being fully who they were outweighed the potential pain of the harsh judgment of others, they told the Truth. For most, this is liberating! For Michelle's friends, she has witnessed the beautiful unfolding of being themselves and loving freely, as they were meant to do—as we are *all* meant to do!

And so, when you are not allowed to love another based on their genitals, what does that even mean? When you die, you *do* know that you don't have any genitals, right? You are a soul as part of a grander Spirit, again, commonly compared as a wave to an ocean. You may be one with the ocean, but you are still YOU, and you maintain the part of you that makes you YOU.

Why not embrace *that* "you" right now, in *this* lifetime, before it's over? Please take some time in meditation today and FEEL what it feels like to be fully you. What innate gifts are you suppressing because of fear, judgment, or retribution? There is no fear, judgment, or retribution from where we stand in the way station and beyond in the higher realms of existence. You only face those illusory emotions in this entry-level existence.

It's all a game, remember? It's a hologram of your inner thoughts. If you believe you will face fear, rejection, and judgment, then indeed you will. If you project support and love and Truth, you will feel all those things in your becoming and unfolding. If you live in an area that doesn't support the higher Truth of you—move. Be with those who lift you up and inspire you and love the "real" you, not the fake version. You will feel the difference, and it's important now to gravitate toward those who raise your vibration exponentially—not just a little bit, but *a lot*. Your world needs this now. Your continued existence depends on it.

No pressure, though…

Chapter 24

Soul Mates

When you live from a position of "soul" vs. being ego driven, you are bound to run into more of your soul mates.

You have a mistaken idea that you only have one true soul mate. This is romantic nonsense. If you believe that you've engaged in many lifetimes—and by now, we sincerely hope you do—you have met many thousands of souls who are now inhabiting new bodies and new life stories, same as you.

When you see one another as energy beings rather than just skin and bones, you will of course be drawn toward each other as your frequencies align. This doesn't always mean that you are supposed to spend your lifetime with this person; it only means they are familiar because you've engaged with them before.

You are all just bumping into each other again for recognition and possibly closure. This doesn't mean if you encounter one that they are a good "forever" partner. Accept the connection for what it is, and check in with how your frequencies match. It may be that you are long lost friends or sworn enemies. The energy may be palpable. Follow it intuitively to where it leads you, but as always, be careful of forming unhealthy attachments. Love freely.

Please understand that your soul may inhabit more than one body at a time, a phenomenon known as a "twin soul" or "twin flame" relationship. Many of you misread this as well. If you meet such a person, it should feel easy and light—not destructive and stressful. It is your very soul inside of another person! There should be *instant* recognition and unconditional love. If you do not currently love yourself, you will draw toward you other soul mates who also do not love themselves. You will learn many lessons this way, and that is alright.

And yet, if you work on loving yourself, if you live a life of service and joy and meditation and peace, you will easily draw toward yourself other parts of your soul, whether in romantic form or via other deep friendships. Conversation will flow, there will be no disagreements. Your energies will be amplified as you align, for your soul knows itself and is delighted to be reunited with itself!

This isn't as common as you'd like, because you haven't done the tools to lead a life of peace and abundance, as laid out in our first two books. If you are living from this place, and you manifest well and often, and you are not only enjoying your life in each moment, but giving out to your neighbors (whom you are one with), you will indeed encounter more soul mates and possibly a twin soul, or even two.

Remember, you are unlimited beings with eternal Light. When you inhabit a body, it only *seems* as if you are limited, but you are *not*. Think of yourself as a soul and you will encounter other souls who share the same vibration more easily, for you all are not encumbered by the density of your material bodies. Imagine it and you will become it, for you already are it—a soul, that is.

It may seem challenging to imagine something you deem "invisible," such as a soul. Yet you may feel it from an energetic standpoint. The more you feel yourself as a soul, the less pain you will have in the body as well. Vibrant health will be a welcome side effect of this! If you insist on only treating the body after it is sick from emotional pain and suffering, this particular lifetime of yours will be a brief one.

Chapter 25

New Year and Snow

It is a new calendar year where Michelle lives in America, and there is renewed hope in the hearts of many.

Michelle, as an empath, can *feel* this hopeful expectancy in the masses, and it makes her feel light and happy.

This morning, she awoke to snow in her small Northern California town, which only happens once or twice a year. This, too, made her feel light and happy.

The point here is that you could ALWAYS feel light and happy. In fact, we encourage it.

Perhaps we should use the word "peaceful," as you tend to use the term "happy" only when you achieve some item or goal that gives you pleasure. Happiness, like snow, is often temporary and fleeting.

The gently falling snow is peaceful to Michelle. It is quiet, and it puts a blanket of white across the many trees in her neighborhood. The world appears, for now, clean and new and problem-less—which is the higher Truth of the way it really is. All you ever need to focus on is your "now." And when the now turns into the next day or the following week, all you ever need to focus on is your NOW.

And in the now, all is clean and new and problem-less. There are no obstacles, no challenges—not even any real "goals" or New Year's resolutions in the now, there is only <u>right now</u>.

What do all of your goals and resolutions, and yes even intentions (as Michelle likes to set this time of year) lead to anyhow? Peace? Happiness? Well-being?

Once you lose the last of the extra pounds you dislike on your body, once you get the job or the lover or the house or the vacation—then what? What is the emotion? Peace, happiness, well-being?

Peace, happiness, and well-being are all a part of the true you, which is made of Love. *The true you needs for nothing. It is whole and complete as it is.* If you can remember that for more than a few moments each day, you will have "won" at the game that is life. Be in the now. Play in the snow. Revel in a new year.

You are a new you in each moment. You create and decide who you want to be in each and every single moment in your so-called time, which is an illusion. Why not decide to be peaceful, happy, whole, complete, exactly as you are?

As we have said, hope is a powerful emotion. It is the turning point toward bliss, which is your birthright. Take the momentum of a new year and run with it.

Chapter 26

By Being Angry at a Person, You Invite them Further into Your Experience

Let's say, for example, that someone provokes you. There are many who feel bored without any sort of drama, and so they revel not in snow, and lightness of being, but in drawing you into their life story through untruths and other sorts of negativity.

When you show any sort of reaction, you are saying "yes" to their invitation. This does not mean you don't care. In fact, we would say it's quite the opposite. *You care enough for your individual peace, and therefore the peace of all mankind, to withdraw your support from their harshness or cruelty.*

When you "unplug" from control dramas, the person on the other end will eventually tire of being out in the cold, so to speak. They will seek and find another who may want to engage, and that is that other person's lesson to learn. *When you make peace a priority, and you show up strong and vibrant in your energy, those others who wish to control and demean you will stop showing up in your environment.*

As this is your game, it is also your arena. Do all those little things each day that keep you light and playful, and you will attract all manner of other souls to your type of "party."

We understand this may not seem as easy as it sounds, but we assure you it is, once you get the hang of it. Soon, the bullies will make you laugh at their attempts to draw you into their soap opera-like shenanigans, and instead of responding with anger, you will maintain your peace, which is what we want for you.

How does this play out at the national level? The same way, of course. Are you beginning to see the connection between the microcosms and macrocosms of our Universe, and how they all coincide and interplay? As you maintain your peace, you not only serve as an example for others in your midst to maintain their own sense of peace, but because we are all connected, you inject peaceful energy into the hearts and minds of everyone else on the planet.

In addition, if you are a leader of a nation, and you have positive intentions of peace and plenty for your country, and you see your particular country as part of the whole world, you would do well to play by the same "rules" we just laid out for you. When you encounter a "bully," as there are many who pride themselves as serving ego and pride before citizens, we ask you to disengage. This may feel as if you are not doing your "job," but it is the exact opposite. You are showing the way, demonstrating the feelings of peace instead of pleading to get your way or to demand others see it the "right" way.

There is no right or wrong, remember? Only your perceptions make it so. When another leader is doing something you deem deplorable, calmly state how you see things and shine your light brightly on the situation. Unite with other leaders of like minds and like souls, and as you gain in numbers (and you will, we promise!) you will attain higher levels of peace, calm, and understanding.

Michelle and Jodah were researching a trip to Indonesia when they somehow began speaking of the Sultan of Brunei. Jodah had worked on one of his many jet planes, and they were discussing how wealthy he was and how he provided free education and healthcare to the poor people of his small country.

And yet, when they explored this further, they discovered many atrocities the sultan had inflicted on these same people. Stories surfaced of corruption and rape and violence, and Michelle and Jodah felt disheartened.

Immediately, Michelle remembered our suggestions and that everything is energy. She shed light heavily upon the situation there, and instead of getting indignant and raging at the atrocities (which would only add to the violent energy directed there) she decided to add healing, hopeful energy to the people of that country, as well as all those on the planet who feel oppressed.

That oppression is heavy victimhood, and you are not helping by being enraged at it! You are then a part of the problem. We realize how much you want to "do" something on this physical planet, and we would like to offer once again the power of your thoughts when directed toward the solution rather than the problem. When you shine a light on oppressed people, you give them the opportunity to rise up on their own, not to fight, but to maintain their peace and gather and unite until there are more peaceful energies on the planet than violent ones. This is NOT a passive process! It is the most powerful thing you can do in each moment, so please pay attention and follow through on our suggestion. *Meditate, visualize light shining on each situation you research or encounter, and observe how things get better.*

In fact, write it down! Document how things get better by your positive intentions and visualizations, and use your social media to broadcast the results of this peace process! More like-minded, like-vibing people will be more likely to join you if you "publish" positive results rather than insisting others see it your way.

Chapter 27

Energy Healing will be the ONLY Healing in the Future

Jodah and Michelle are hurting.

Michelle's stomach and digestion continue to give her physical pain and discomfort, and Jodah's neck and shoulder continue to render him unable to perform his work duties.

As an empath, Michelle is also taking on Jodah's pain; she is feeling the same pain on her left side as Jodah, her twin soul, is feeling on his right.

Michelle knows what is happening, and yet the pain continues, despite all of her attempts to rid herself of the pain. Jodah also is aware of his emotional contributions to his physical pain, and yet both of them continue to suffer.

Michelle is a certified Reiki master—a Japanese form of energy healing. She has been giving herself and Jodah this form of energy healing, and yet, the results have been less than appealing.

We would like to offer that they are simply trying too hard to gain a result (becoming pain free) after lots of momentum toward what they do *not* want.

Do you do this as well?

For example, when you want more money, is your focus on your lack of money? If you want a lover, is your focus on how you don't have one yet?

For many years, Michelle focused more on being a victim than on being powerful. Because of this orientation, many others took advantage of her feeling nature. She found herself caught up in several control dramas that she could not explain. Her energy attracted it, and because she practiced that vibrational offering of "poor me" for several years, it is taking several more years to "undo" that practiced vibration.

Jodah is also feeling trapped, but in a different way. His frequency is more attuned to assisting us in our mission to teach peace than designing aircraft, as has been his means of income for several decades. But that is a lot of momentum to slow down all at once! While he stays focused on how much he does NOT want to do this line of work any longer, he is getting in his own way toward the path of freedom. He knows this on an intellectual level, and yet he feels *powerless* to stop it. So in this way, he is also projecting a victim mentality, and the new life he envisions of freedom and adventure and travel stays in the distance.

The trick in this—and it is really not a "trick" at all—is to stop overthinking the situation! Take a time out, and revel in nature or some other such pleasure that lifts your spirits, and continue visualizing the outcome. As Michelle and Jodah are intimately connected and their souls are entwined, they may envision this for each other, creating a more powerful force. You may also do this for one another, envisioning a positive outcome, as we have suggested in past chapters. There is less of a tendency to focus on the lack when it is another's vision, and so your positive vibrational offering is more constant and therefore effective.

Chapter 28

Be Careful and Deliberate with your Thoughts and Actions

This is very important for the most impact! We know we just said to stop overthinking things, but as long as you are in a body, you are going to have thoughts in order to turn them into things. That is what you signed up for, remember?

And so, when a thought surfaces that emulates what you do NOT want, wipe it away quickly and offer a new thought that emulates your growth and expansion. This is the most powerful peace process you will ever learn, and once you do this in great numbers, your world will take a giant leap toward the highest forms of spiritual evolution!

You will know you are suppressing your innate power when the things and experiences that are showing up for you are unwanted. It is at this time where a pivoting process is crucial, for you simply spin around on your heels (this is a metaphor) and go in the complete opposite direction! Be sure in your innate power, knowing the strength of your soul and your connection to Spirit, and offer up vibrations of peace, harmonizing your Self to others of the same "tone."

You can do this.

Try using the affirmation: "It's all coming together now."

Say it over and over again until you feel it happening.

"It's all coming together now."

Say it until you see "signs" of things coming together for you, both miracles and manifestations, as well as an uplifting of your spirits.

"It's all coming together now."

Say it when times are "good," as well as in times when you are in physical or emotional pain. You will rise in vibration while you are saying this, and even a little lift in frequency helps.

"It's all coming together now."

Say it until you see results in your community and the world at large. If you don't believe you can affect the world at large, please go back and reread our earlier books. You are powerful—all of you! Come together.

Believe that you are *all* coming together now.

Affirm: "Everyone and everything is coming together now."

Ooh, doesn't THAT feel good now? Say it again. Out loud if you can.

"Everyone and everything is coming together now."

Do you feel it now? Do you feel a difference in the "force," the energy surrounding you? Do you feel an "upliftment"? Yes, we know we just created a new word for you.

Please continue affirming until you feel a difference, until you know things have changed permanently for the better.

And then rest, for you are still within a body. Allow your body to renew its life-force energy—and it will.

Chapter 29

From Me to We to Me Again

When you switch from "me" to "we" thinking, in other words from the individual to the collective, you tap into a larger flow of health, wealth, and abundance that returns to you tenfold. We've discussed this before—it's circular. It all comes back to you, like a boomerang.

Many of you haven't learned this, and you continue to hoard your good, your manifestations, as if that is all you are ever going to receive. Limited thinking will garner a limited supply that will eventually run out.

When you understand that you come from *limitless expansion*, your good goes on and on and on, and you may receive it just as soon as you match the frequency of it.

If "it," meaning all the good stuff—things, opportunities, adventures, etc.—*still* isn't showing up for you, know that you must heal yourself in order to heal all others (again, you are all connected).

This healing is a simpler process than you currently believe. When you become still, whatever surfaces, look at it, then let it go. Do this over and over again.

Michelle is currently going over the changes her editor presented for our last book. The editing software they both use shows when the editor has offered either an insertion or a deletion of words, as well as notes on the side about where there is confusion. Michelle, as the presumed author, has the authority to either accept the insertion or delete the insertion. She can accept or reject each deletion. She has been doing this all day long, over and over again, and it occurred to her that *life is much the same way.*

When your life story presents something to you—either a change or another's behavior toward you, or a situation you believe you didn't ask for (you did energetically or it wouldn't be showing up), you have the choice to accept or delete.

We offer that the best way to deal with anything that surfaces for you is to first accept, and THEN delete.

For example, Michelle and Jodah both know that their physical pains are surfacing due to unwanted situations. Both are resisting the changes immensely. And when there is a LOT of resistance against something, it creates dammed-up pain. If they could accept their respective situations *as is*, then delete, the dam would burst forth with all the things, experiences, and adventures they've been keeping at bay.

There doesn't *always* have to be a lesson learned. The lesson may come later, but certainly not in the midst of the painful situation, whatever that might be. *The pain comes from the energetic discrepancy.*

If you already have one foot in the door of what you want, but you believe someone or something else is holding you back, you are between two "channels" of reality. The Truth is no one can *ever* hold you back but you.

Please hear this again: No one can ever hold you back but you.

Yes, the energetic discrepancy can be painful, but you choose whether or not to accept, then delete. You choose when and how to let go.

When you let go, you are free. How do you let go? By stopping yourself with the absurd assumption that you can control everything and everyone. You can't. Not with most things.

What you have control over is your mind. When you meditate more and clear yourself of unnecessary and negative judgments, you will live in a world of peace that you created. And as we have pointed out, it is that peace that we wish for you—all 7 billion of you.

And yet, when you meditate more and come from a clear place, you will know it is time to leave a situation in which you are no longer growing. It will not feel good, as you are in a better feeling place now and that situation—whether it is a job or a relationship—will no longer feel good.

When the thoughts "this doesn't feel good" or "I don't want this," surface, know that the Universe only hears "feel good" and "want this," if the Universe had ears, that is.

There is no negation in all the Universe. As we've said before, and which bears repeating, you must be deliberate in your thoughts and actions. While it's good to accept that something doesn't feel good, be open during the transition time of not knowing what it is you want to "fill the gap" with before you can let the old situation fall away or be deleted.

Does this make sense to you? Accept, then delete. Accept, then delete.

For example: a friend of Michelle and Jodah's recently got a head cold over the holidays. The friend said she bragged that she "never got sick," and then she did and it was awful. She suffered because she didn't want it, especially because it went against her plans. But as she was choosing her words to speak aloud, the only thing the Universe heard her say was "get sick." Sickness was the energetic vibration she was giving out, along with a lack of rest for the body, and so sickness was what she received.

You can do this with any unwanted situation, you see. If your bank account is empty and that is something unwanted, and if you are telling your friends (and yourself by obsessing about it in your head) that you are "broke" (what an unfortunate choice of words), and you are focusing on the *lack* of money and/or *lack* of ideal job, more of THAT will keep showing up. It's science, that's all it is.

Divert your attention to something enjoyable. Give yourself time to rest, then inspire yourself by doing pleasurable activities that soothe your soul. Allow for meditation and imagination—dream big and well and often. Research ideal jobs, travel, and charities when you start feeling a little better and stop obsessing so much. As the "tide turns," and you are flowing more toward feeling better than resisting what is, you'll begin receiving intuitive "hits" that are like striking gold!

Act on these intuitive, inspired ideas! That's where all innovation comes from.

When you've gone from accepting, to deleting, to moving forward, you've completed the cycle, and you are healing others by healing yourself. The more often you do this, the less an unwanted situation will affect you. You will not get attached to the outcome; instead, you will acknowledge what is occurring, delete it from your mind (imagine wiping it away with a cloth or sponge), then imagining and innovating.

Jodah doesn't want his shoulder, neck, and arm pain. He doesn't want to face that his body is rebelling by not letting him work. He manifested this by chronic thoughts of not wanting to do this line of work any longer. His arm was like a donkey refusing to go another step farther down the path.

Michelle doesn't want this conflict with her teen daughter. She takes it personally and worries incessantly about her. She is suffering and sending fearful energy out, and then wonders why it shows up as stomach pain (lack of control).

If Jodah could accept—not just intellectually, but emotionally—that this physical situation is just a construct of his mind, and that he can accept, delete, rest, inspire, imagine, innovate, the physical pain will eventually go away. It has to. It will be of a differing frequency. *That's how you change the channel.*

If Michelle could accept that her daughter is following her own path and that she is learning individual lessons that have nothing to do with her, she, too, could change the channel. Her daughter is—in psychological terms—individuating, while Michelle is in a different vibrational setting of moving from "me" to "we" thinking, as we discussed when we began this section. Her teenager is at the appropriate level of her evolution, as is Michelle. They are just currently at opposing ends of the spectrum.

Many others stay "stuck" at the individuation stage of evolution. It is an appropriate and healthy thing to do, but it is our hope that you come back around to embracing a more all-encompassing version of reality that includes all.

Chapter 30

You All Want Different Things

You are one with all that you see and hear. Their choices are your choices and simply prove the diversity of things.

On some of the television shows Michelle enjoys, such as *Celebrity Wife Swap, Extreme Homes,* and *International House Hunters,* she sees examples of how you all want different things to be happy.

You encounter this every day, don't you? Whether it is your spouse who disagrees about what type of house you should live in, or a friend who doesn't appreciate your sense of clothing style, or a family member who doesn't understand your creative home decorations, it is a fascinating experience to witness how different our tastes can be!

If everyone wanted the same things, there would be a shortage of all the "good" stuff. But since everyone deems "good" and "bad" differently, one person's good is another person's awful. This makes life colorful for you, and it is what you signed up for! If your partner does not agree with you, often you are forced to make compromises and sometimes get in control dramas, as we have discussed previously.

It is easiest if you surround yourself with like-minded, like-vibing others in the first place, so you do not have these struggles. And yet, even the most similar temperaments will disagree on some things, especially if they are important to you.

If it feels crucial to your well-being to have your way, perhaps you are taking the creative choices offered to you too seriously. If you are continually suppressing your true desires to please an overbearing partner, you might want to look at why you are staying with each other if you no longer make each other happy.

Continually compromising your true desires is not a good way to live and causes unnecessary suffering.

A true, loving partnership will honor and respect each person's creative differences, and make some allowances and adjustments accordingly.

The same holds true for nations, cultures, and customs. What one country deems important can be far different than another's, yes? And yet, they are like a quilt of many colors. As long as no one is being violent, you may learn to respect one another's societal beliefs without war and disharmony. But it starts with you, as all things do.

Chapter 31

Source Doesn't Care if You Individuate

Separation is all an illusion. As you focus more on the ego's creative diversity rather than the larger part of you that is Spirit, Source energy will continue to shine on and love you anyway.

Michelle awoke in the middle of the night unable to return to sleep. Her mind was focused on all the things she deemed "wrong" in her life, from her teen daughter's absence on her birthday to her health (she was suffering from a migraine) and the extra weight she put on over the holidays. As she was tired and her body was in pain, her mind began spiraling to more "bad" things, until she knew she had to stop the cycle from triggering her into an even deeper, lonelier, pain-filled space.

It occurred to her that in the same way Source shines on her and loves her as she individuates and creates a life that is "hers," she can learn to do the same for her daughter. Michelle imagined her shiny Self as large and bright, then she affirmed over and over again: "I am one with Source energy" until the pain subsided and she returned to sleep.

Anytime your mind turns obsessive over negative thoughts, or if you are feeling fear or anxiety or resentment or anger or dread, throw your mind a "bone" to chew on with a positive affirmation such as the one above. Your mind is like a dog that needs diversion from time to time while it's still training. Reminding yourself who you really are is a way to escape the suffering you cause yourself on earth.

Chapter 32

Turn Chronic Worry into Joy

You may turn chronic states of worry into incessant—or constant—states of joy. It's just a flip of the coin, really.

When you are feeling anxious, underneath that unpleasant emotion lies fear and doubt and worry. You are literally creating your worst nightmare as you continue to experience all the negative charge of this particular frequency.

We are not saying to reject your worries. Quite the opposite. We are encouraging you instead to give those worries and fears a good long look—stare your fears in the face, and as we've said before and will repeat until you download it into your brain's framework—release it, rapidly.

Your fears are unwarranted. Always.

Yes, you might die. And when you die, you will return to a glorious space where you have no physical or emotional pain.

And so, if the worst you can imagine is that you will die, that fear is unwarranted.

Your other fears and worries tend to revolve around some sort of judgment, yes?

Again, when you leave this lifetime behind and no longer carry around a body, there will be nothing to judge, agreed? You will not compete against who has the better body or job or spouse or children. Therefore, in Spiritual form, which is your true nature, there is nothing to fear.

And so, the next time you find yourself in a state of worry and anxiety, usually marked by a more rapid heartbeat, insomnia, tense muscles, etc., please stop and ask yourself the following questions:

"Am I dying?"

The answer is always yes, for everyone on your planet will die at some point, yes? So let's get clearer now.

"Am I going to die in this instant?"

If the answer is yes, be at peace knowing the direction you are headed is into unconditional love and bliss.

If the answer is no, please ask yourself, your inner being, if you feel as if you are being judged—or that if you go forward with your plans, will you be judged in the future?

How does that judgment feel? Have you ever judged another? How did *that* feel?

Does any of this judgment matter? Do you want it to matter? Because if you choose to continue this line of thinking, you will make thought into matter, because as we've said before over and over again, you are all CREATORS.

Spirit *never* judges, and you are mostly Spirit in human form. When you die, none of this judgment and competition and comparison stuff matters any longer.

Choose to be this way now. What is the opposite word for judgment for you—in your own words? Be that now.

We might choose your word "compassion." Perhaps "try on" compassion today, and see how *that* feels vs. how you feel when you are filled with worry and anxiety and doubt and depression.

As the depression begins to lift, make sure you amplify that newer, lighter feeling x10 or maybe even x100! That's how you begin the process of spiraling upward into a new way of life, into a lifestyle filled with magnified living—what you may call miracles and magic, and what we consider Truth.

Chapter 33

If You Don't Believe You Can Fly, You Won't

Turkeys don't fly much, do they? You could say it's because their bodies are too heavy for their wings, but the same is true for bees, and they fly.

It is always, always, always your belief that makes it so.

If you want your team to win, see them triumphant. If you yell and scream at their every loss and misstep, they will create more mistakes.

Everything is energy, and so if you can start to see it before you believe it, seeing it will make it so.

We are not saying, "Don't be on the front lines," when you feel called to do so. It is good to travel and feed and clothe and shelter and treat the illnesses of your brothers and sisters, when possible.

But your energetic offering is *crucial*—and you can do it from anywhere in the world. All great leaders performed miracles in this way. Jesus turned water into wine and healed the sick because he believed he could. Many great yogis have performed fabulous feats, such as not breathing, sleeping, or eating for long periods of time, because they spent lots of time in meditation and believed they could do these seemingly impossible things.

Try this: when you share with a like-minded, like-vibing friend that you intend to achieve your society's version of "impossible," give them two "high-five" hand claps, for that equals 10 and will remind you to amplify your energetic offering of this times 10! The energy of clapping hands makes things happen, and it is fun. Try it sometime.

And if you do find your calling is to physically travel to help others, please do so out of a sense of compassion and oneness toward all beings. Do not go with a sense of obligation or righteousness, but because you are taking inspired action on your heart's whisperings.

If you feel called to protest or fight something, please take a step back and see exactly what you are doing instead—lending your energy toward the exact thing that is unwanted! Don't add any momentum at all toward violent thought or action. Stop the flow of that now, and eventually, it must cease. Stop and focus your Light on the situation, and watch what happens. Again, this is not passive—it's the single most *active* thing you can do!

Chapter 34

Gilded Everything

Imagine everything as golden. If alchemy in medieval times was turning base metals into gold, then in modern times, we want you to play with this form of alchemical transformation with various situations you are now facing.

We have spoken of alchemy in our last book, *Peace is Power*, but now we want you to take it a step further. We have also had you pour Light onto a difficult situation, a perceived problem, or perhaps even something you'd like to make manifest into your life, such as a new job, home, or relationship.

We hope you've enjoyed great success using your access to your inner Light to transform any situation! And now, some situations that remain could still use your active imagination.

These are the issues Michelle believes she is facing. Some of them are not even her own, but as she is an empath, she continues to take them on and make them her problems.

Her parents are elderly and sick. They are creating vicious rumors about her that are complete fabrications, and they are attempting to pit other family members, such as her beloved sister, against her.

At first, when she learned of the ridiculous accusations, she laughed. The lies were so outrageous that she felt pity on them, then moved on and enjoyed a wonderful evening playing board games with her sister when the power went out during a big storm. Ironically, the storm brewing outside mimicked the internal storm that was forming for her!

The following day, Michelle was tired. Her studio roof had leaked and destroyed some of her belongings. She knew that it was only stuff, and yet she was tired. Now, from a tired state, she began to get angry at the accusations, feeling powerless about fighting them. Michelle does not like being in a defensive position.

And because she put herself in this position, rather than ignoring the rantings of angry, toxic people, she started spiraling into a dark hole. In trying to divert her attention to something else, she watched television, and only could find the first press conference of a president whom she despised.

Can you see how hate travels?

Michelle knew this was happening, and as she talked about it with Jodah in the hot tub, she decided to give herself a day to fully feel all her negative emotions about the original issue—her parents' lies. She decided to cry, be mad, and "try that on" for a while, until it just didn't feel good anymore at all. So she went to bed.

This morning is a new day. She has decided to let this go. If she attempted to confront her parents and say that their accusations are ridiculous and untrue, they would get what they wanted to begin with—a reaction. Instead, she said "rise" dozens of times as she rose, then she meditated some, and came to her desk to allow us to write through her, and in doing so, elevated her current vibrational offering.

Now, she could have chosen to join in on the rage. And if she did, she would join the collective *un*-consciousness that brews beneath the surface of those who choose to continue the path of anger and violence. Again, we are not saying to ignore your feelings! They are important indicators of where you are emotionally. But you can turn things around faster and faster the more often you recognize what is happening sooner, and turn the flood of emotions toward goodness and Light.

Michelle is now imagining her parents covered in gold. She sees her sister, who had her back, also gilded. She pours gold over her teen daughter, whom she is meeting this weekend after seeing that conflict covered in Light! And she sees her eldest daughter, who is travelling out of the country next week with a new friend, enjoying gold-encased adventures everywhere she goes!

Now, moving forward out of rage and fear and resentment, and into a higher place of learned wisdom, this gilded stuff is getting fun! Michelle feels like the old story of King Midas, without all the negative parts of the old tale. Michelle is creating a new fairytale, and she continues seeing Jodah's hurt neck and shoulder covered in gold now, and she sees her books all shiny and gilded, and she pours gold over her new TV reality show pitch: "Don't Change the Channel." (Update: The TV show is now in development with Black Rock Entertainment!)

As she imagines gold-covered experiences and opportunities, more and more come to her on their own. Offers to lead talks on cruise ships and more workshops around the world, all-expense paid! (Update: Michelle is getting invites almost daily to speak through various groups!) Michelle sees the entire world now encased in gold, including the president who she does not resonate with, for now she knows the power of covering ALL in Light and gold...

You can try this today. It is a fun exercise in faith and trust and growing into your next best Self. If you still have a problem with allowing good things into your life, such as the energy of money, then please go back and read our other books.

CHAPTER 35

The Absence of Resistance is Elation

Michelle's publisher asked her to write about how she felt after her very first session with us. When she said she felt amazing, he wanted more descriptions. And yet, in the absence of any resistant emotion from her—the state in which she needs to be in order to transmit and communicate with us—there is nothing but elation.

We are bliss. We are surrounded by bliss. You have your moments of such feelings now, but they are fleeting. As we've stated in our previous books, you may experience longer, and more pleasurable states of elation and bliss the more time you spend in meditation and nature, and perhaps reading our books or attending our events, or that of another high-vibrational spiritual teacher.

When you leave this bodily existence, you will know only bliss. It is part of why we came here to teach you now, because you are getting more and more glimpses into it! And yet, you could not dwell in it permanently from where you are now, or your dense body vehicle would explode. You must raise your vibration incrementally each new day, as we have instructed.

An easier way to rise to an elevated state is simply to have no reactions at all to anything. Some would say that is denial, and we would counter *no*. If you have truly been practicing our teachings, accepting whatever has happened and deleting as quickly as possible, you may complete this process more rapidly merely by remaining a wide open channel of compassion and grace.

It is as it is on your Facebook page—if someone is posting things on your "wall" that you do not resonate with, you may simply press the button to "unfriend" or even block them. You may do the same in life, only you don't just press a button. Let it go, then gravitate toward others who lift you up, not tear you down.

For example, Michelle had an acquaintance through social media whom she had known long ago in high school. This person liked to "argue" with everything Michelle posted. Michelle believes that everyone has a right to their opinion, so she let her "stay." That is, until she began an argument over a beautifully written post on compassion.

Who can fight with the word "compassion"? Michelle said it is her belief that compassion means "oneness" and brings unity. This person started going in a downward-spiraling direction, indicating that some people are just "evil" and that "Satan" leads them. She continued that some people do not deserve our compassion, and that that is naïve and dangerous thinking.

At this point, Michelle unfriended and blocked her acquaintance. As we stated scientifically in *Peace is Power*, just as there is no such thing as "cold"—only an absence of heat, there is no such thing as "evil" in the absence of Light—only darkness. To "undo" darkness, you must simply turn on the Light.

Just as Michelle believes as we do that God is not a person, but a flow toward ever-increasing and positive GOODNESS, she also does not believe that "Satan" is a person. You may fight us on this, but there is no such thing as an active force for evil. When you are in the "dark," you are simply rejecting the Light.

Let's think about this now: do you really believe a little man in a red suit with horns and a pitch fork is egging you on to do bad things to others?

That image is a caricature, an easy way to point blame on another instead of accepting that we are all one, all connected, and taking responsibility for our own actions as a means toward uniting with the whole.

Nothing is forcing you or another to do wrong. You all have free will. If you choose to eat badly, no one is doing that to you, you are doing it to yourself. If someone steals from you, think for a moment where that person might be coming from? If that were you, and you were poor or hungry or destitute, what would *you* do? That is the practice of compassion—knowing the suffering of others as that of your own experience, without making suffering a competition of sorts. (As we note elsewhere in this book, the original Latin meaning of "compassion" is "to love together with.")

This other person on Facebook went on to say that Michelle did not know evil, and therefore the former friend was "right."

Who has *not* known darkness? As long as you've lived on this planet, in the firm denseness of this reality, you've felt the contrast. You can get mired in it, and make a contest out of who has suffered the most from whatever story you created pre-birth, *or you can learn your lessons until you don't have to any longer.*

Michelle could not explain all of this in a social media post, so she deleted it. So should you. *You do not ever have to explain yourself to others.* Shine your Light for all to see, and if those in your midst are blinded, they will leave or you can move away from them. If they shine right along with you, those are your people.

What can you do for those who believe in evil? You cannot fight their belief systems. You cannot fight their wars with or for them—in fact, we would highly recommend against it! In the belief of a force of evil or a vengeful demon, who can take the blame for your wrongdoings? You are supporting evil and violence! That may not be your intention, but whatever you focus on grows, remember?

Believe in goodness, and you will live in a good world. Believe in forward-moving growth and expansion, and you will move right along with it, toward joys unknown and unheard of at this moment. This is not naiveté, it is higher wisdom. You cannot explain this to someone not ready to receive it. You can live it, and they will either fall in line with you, or leave.

Naiveté is believing in a red devil or a judgmental man in white robes in the sky. You will know the Truth when you leave this life behind. Michelle got a glimpse of the way station when she had a near death experience, but you can have a spiritually transcendent experience while you are still here if you actively engage in the flow of better-feeling thoughts, people, and experiences.

Chapter 36

Taking Inventory

We realize that we have asked you to do this in prior books, but this is a good place in this book for you to assess past manifestations since your last reading, and how they made you feel. Use the gift of memory to cherish and focus on the good stuff. For example, in the past year, Michelle has manifested an RV, a hot tub, a new sports car, an all-expense trip to Cancun, a book deal, an oracle card app deal, a potential television deal, a healthier body, a new mattress and headboard, and paid opportunities to speak throughout California. Those things and experiences made her feel free, creative, vibrant, and excited! She is currently bringing into her reality (and she left out the "hows" of it, of course) new, larger bedroom drawers and a lakefront property. She's visualizing those things daily; as she puts away her clothes, she imagines putting them in the larger drawers she wants rather than the drawers she's had since she was 13 years old that are small and outdated. Rather than complaining or being irritated by the old drawers, she simply imagines the new ones, without dwelling on the fact that they are not there physically with her yet! She knows it can happen in the blink of an eye, based on her past manifestation assessment. That is why we have you do an assessment first! (Update: Michelle commissioned an artist to refurbish a set of bedroom dresser drawers! They are larger than her original vision, and manifested more creatively than just purchasing them.)

The same is true for her lakefront property. When she performs errands in the neighboring town she desires to live in, she drives past the lot she desires and pretends as if she were driving home. She sits in her car, gazing at the serene beauty of the lake, and feels fulfilled, tranquil, and at peace. Then she goes home and does other things that are fulfilling and that make her feel the same level of serenity and peace. For her, that is writing and doing yoga and meditating.

You all know this by now, we hope. Sometimes, you forget, and that is okay. We just wish to keep you on track with your manifestations. One way that Michelle can get her drawers and property more quickly is to give more. Then she will be in the energy of unlimitedness, which is the Truth of who she is, as are you. Give today, and watch how rapidly your new desires go from thought into form! Have fun with this, and give from a pure heart, not out of obligation, but from a place of wanting what's best for others, which only boomerangs back at you.

Chapter 37

PerSEVERance

Google would say that this word is defined the following way:
1. steadfastness in doing something despite difficulty or delay in achieving success.

The original meaning of perseverance is from Latin, meaning, "abiding by strictly."

We bring this up now because we do not want for you to be "strict" about anything whatsoever! To create what it is you want, *sever* any cords holding you back by imagining the flow more than the blockage.

The middle portion of the word is indeed "sever." And so, in order to continue with whatever mission you are on at the moment, please undo the alleged block, as we have stated in previous books, and turn toward what it is you DO want. Strict discipline is the same as "forcing" something to happen! Do that, and you'll keep pushing what it is you want AWAY from you, not toward you, you see. You've experienced this before—have you learned?

Stay in the flow of good things, and soon you will have and experience them! Continue on, despite what surfaces. Go around the challenges that surface—how you might in a video game—for remember, this is all just a game anyhow! Perseverance is "hard," and we believe living should be full of ease and grace and flow.

Chapter 38

Share What You are Learning

Rather than telling others what it is you believe, try sharing what it is you are currently learning from your life experiences. Please remember, your beliefs are just thoughts you think over and over again obsessively until you *think* they become who you are. Nothing could be farther from the Truth! You are so much more than you *think* you are, and most of your thoughts have been fed to you since birth from your family, your society, your culture, the news, etc.

You are Divine. You are scientifically a being of pure Light! You are Love that is currently in dense form in order to create and grow. And so, please show how you are creating and expanding…when others complain, instead of sinking to their energetic wavelength, try sharing: "This is what I am learning right now…" or "I am reading this book or taking this class or trying this approach, and *this* is what it is teaching me."

Most likely they will offer a retort, and that is okay. You can either engage in more thoughtful discussions, or you can discard their opinions about what *they* think of what *you* are learning. It doesn't matter, because it's *your* path, and they can expand *with* you, offer their own methods of expansion, or discard your teachings and leave you alone. Whichever way this leans, you are still learning and growing and expanding, yes?

Again, the Universe is always in a state of movement and expansion, and so, standing still will garner illness and stagnation. If you have nothing to share with another about your learning process or current creative pursuits, please find some. This is not difficult. Find an endeavor that makes your heart feel light and happy, like a song. We've encouraged this in the past, and yet, maybe it's time you sought something new—or alternately, allowed a new way of thinking into your life?

Affirm that you are open to receiving a new path of discovery, and the way will be shown.

Chapter 39

Positive Outcome

Yesterday, Michelle woke up with another migraine. It was considered an important, momentous day for her because her teen daughter had said yes to lunch and shopping after six months of little contact. And so, Michelle lifted her vibrations in the way she has been taught, knowing that the manifestation of the migraine was putting fear into form, and she knew how to rise above it now.

On the long drive over to where her daughter resides with her father, Michelle saw numerous signs that she was on the right path toward peace, not fear. She noted three bulletin boards in a row with the messages "Freedom for All," "Whatever Your Mountain, Climb it Now," and "Do it Now." She figured that the "mountain" was her fear and resentment surrounding the conflict between her and her daughter, and it was definitely time to climb (face) it now! She felt ready.

And as she felt ready, she saw numerous license plates with repeating numbers that signified to her that angels and spirit guides (including us!) were in her midst. She saw the overflowing lakes and rivers, where once there was drought, reminding her to fill herself first, then allow all that goodness and bounty to flow forward for everyone.

She had the thought that every soul is deserving, even if you deem them "evil" or "less than." From the vantage point of Spirit, we are all equal.

And so, as she went into her afternoon with her daughter, all went well. She expected a positive outcome—she even asked aloud for one—and not only did she receive one, it was spelled out for her.

Michelle and her daughter enjoyed lunch and lots of pleasant conversation. They went shopping, and Michelle stood in awe as she watched her daughter give out the various food gift cards she had received as Christmas and birthday gifts to homeless mothers with children on the streets. Inspired, Michelle also gave money to another soul who asked for assistance in going to his basketball tournament. And because she knows that as others succeed, we all do, she gave him what he needed.

Later, Michelle asked her daughter what the message was inside the fortune-telling bath bomb she'd given her daughter for Christmas (kind of like a fortune cookie message). Her daughter showed it to her. It read: POSITIVE OUTCOME

You see, you receive what it is you ask for, always. It may not instantly materialize the way it does in the way station, but as you practice the various tools we lay out for you—such as envisioning the situation bathed in Light and/or in gold—you will always find peace and understanding.

You may think that a mother-daughter conflict is not the same as a nation-to-nation war, but it is. Everything is connected, and what you resolve on a smaller level reflects on a larger one! Resolve the perceived problems you have on the individual and relationship levels, and you will know how powerful it is to alter the outcome via energy, rather than force. In this way, you will one day know peace on your planet.

Where are your current conflicts, on an interpersonal or collective level as a nation? Can you envision a positive outcome and release the details? Can you envision the situation bathed in Light and poured gold? There will be many more tools such as these to propel your newfound peace forward into new heights.

Chapter 40

Man is Frozen

Man—as in hu-man—is in a state of being frozen in time. Because you are more space than matter, more Light than darkness, more energy than emptiness, your density while in a body creates the illusion of being stuck.

As we have noted, there is no such thing as time. And yet, everything appears to slow down when you are within the confines of a body, yes? It's as if instead of scuba diving under water, you were in a larger, more cumbersome submarine.

You are more like the water than you are the submarine. While you still identify with the submarine, you will feel frozen and suffer immensely.

Recognize that the rest of you is always in perpetual motion—from your cells to your soul to the planets. If you can remember the higher Truth of your existence, you will feel lighter and freer. When you feel more light and free, you will engage with the higher frequencies that bring you immense joy, and you will begin to move beyond desiring the earthly pleasures that you have been so good at gathering up until this point.

Not gathering pleasurable things and experiences through the power of your thoughts and feeling vibrations? Please go back and read our first two books until you do. You came here to create, and then allow for those creations to overflow toward all creatures. *This* is your shared purpose as human beings, for you are all connected and came here for the adventure. As you remember more, you will see more flow into your awareness. As you do, please document your treasures so that others may see that it is possible to create a "bounty" of whatever it is you want through the "mere"—and it isn't "small" at all—offering of your energetic vibration.

More be-ing, less do-ing. That is how you move out of a seemingly "frozen" state of existence, and beyond into the higher realms. That is how you follow the Law of Propulsion, which will skyrocket you into perfect well-being.

Chapter 41

Energy Escalation

Have you ever felt the anger in a room escalate in an argument? You can feel that same anger raise in resistance when you protest something or someone—you are literally guaranteeing the opposite of what you want by being in an opposing state of resistance to what is.

Stand instead in solidarity.

Envision a positive outcome for all. Drip it in gold and shine a Light on it together in *unity*. You are then moving humanity forward, not backward, energetically—which is what matters, ironically. It's all there is.

Calmly and firmly state your case from your limited perspective when communication is necessary. Yet words and even actions can only do so much. *The power of peace is in your energetic surrendering.*

Michelle wants to join a Women's March in Sacramento to join energetic forces with thousands of women across the United States toward the empowerment of women. This falls—not coincidentally—the day after the presidential inauguration to swear in a man who has said many derogatory statements about women.

If the march is an effort to unite forces and rain Light upon the situation, this will affect not only the president, but anyone who believes someone is "less than" based on their skin color or genitals or sexual orientation. And yet, there are many who are angry at the president and what he represents, and gathering in protest could only serve to raise the overall level of animosity in the area, and in the nation—even the world.

That is not their intention. The women who gather do so out of a feeling of powerlessness and wanting to just DO something to stop this man from "ruining" the progress women have made over the centuries. From where we stand, it is ridiculous to identify with the body so much that you think one "kind" of body vehicle is better than another. This is another form of judgment, comparison, and competition. It's what gets you all in trouble and incites violence.

Instead, try seeing yourself as a soul—a skinless, genital-less, energy source that is expansive and beautiful in its purity. You are all THAT. Try the "unzipping" your body visualization exercise we gave you in our first book, and if you choose to join in on a "march," instead of seeing it as a protest, imagine everyone there "unzipping" their bodies and envision their pure souls in all their glory.

Then connect their soul to yours.

In this way, you will create a chain of souls in a mission to remember the Truth of who you are! Instead of joining a "resistance" movement, which we've established only creates pain and suffering, move humanity FORWARD exponentially by seeing only energy. In seeing energy, in pouring Light and gold over insufferable situations, you will know peace. And when *you* know peace, peace will spread.

Chapter 42

Everything Fits Now

Michelle was "running errands," as you say, and had the thought, "everything fits now."

When you see *running themes* throughout your life's story, you can often take a moment to summarize, based on the recurring signs.

You have a saying in America that you can't fit a square peg into a round hole. And yet, you try quite often. Another cliché saying of yours: "If it doesn't open, it's not your door."

When you vibrate at the right frequency of your desires, life flows and is *easy*. Life is *supposed* to be EASY—we keep telling you that, and yet, you seem to like a challenge.

Challenges are fine unless they over-stress you and tax the body. If you feel as if you are aligned and ignited on a mission or creative project—that is pure propulsion! It's what we encourage. And yet, if the opposite is true, and you continue finding "blocks" to your success and spiritual evolution, either the alleged "block" is in you and your fears or insecurities, or it simply isn't the path that lights you up.

We've said before, if it doesn't light you up, don't do it. It's that easy. When you are inspired, life takes flight. When you are not, it drags. Don't drag.

Michelle's simple signs were getting her new glasses adjusted to fit her face so that they wouldn't fall off, and allowing the dentist to drill her new crown so that it would fit her mouth and not cause her gums to swell.

The third sign was that after faithfully following her new year's cleanse, her body once again fits into her favorite clothes.

"Everything fits," she thought.

And then she thought of the things in her life that currently are NOT fitting, that she is attempting to "force" instead of allow in their own timing, when her energetic vibration lifts and rises to the occasion. Your mind, when it reaches conclusions about things, often goes toward their contrasting opposite. And that is okay, as long as it allows a *new* idea to form and be birthed.

Michelle is trying to get on local television morning programs that she has been on before, but has received no response. She wants to fill our upcoming workshop, and she is visualizing the full house appropriately, but there's a part of her ego that is still trying to control the situation.

We would advise her, and you, if you find yourself doing the same thing in other matters, to simply do the work required to get the attention of what you desire (i.e., emailing the television producers) and then diverting your attention somewhere else. Do something completely distracting and the opposite of what it is you are trying to *force* into becoming. Force never, ever works, remember? (Update: A friend contacted the station for Michelle. A TV news reporter interviewed Michelle last weekend about our new book and local workshop—she had only one slot left the morning of our workshop!)

Picture, then allow. Picture, then allow. Perhaps ask like-minded others to picture it with you, as the more of you lending your Light on the matter, the more likely it is to come to you sooner rather than later, but then again, there is no such thing as time.

Enjoy the process of delivery. It may come to you in other ways if you let it. Michelle had no idea how she would get her new reality TV show concept into the hands of someone who could pitch it to a big network until she received some random requests from producers on social media. One in particular who aligned with her idea reached out to her, and now she has a phone meeting with him on Monday! (Update: The producer loved the pitch! Michelle and Jodah met with him in Los Angeles, and they are now pitching the TV show to the big networks!)

Let it go, and pay attention to what shows up on your radar. Respond only when you feel inspired to do so, as your inspiration is energetic confirmation that you're definitely on the right track forward.

Chapter 43

Expansion Carries Vibrations Forward

As you continue to grow and expand *with* the natural flow of the creative Universe of which you are a part, that expansion will take on a momentum of its own and carry your vibrations—and those with whom you surround yourself—like a tidal wave carries the ocean.

YOU have that kind of immense power inside of you! Don't you see it now? Doesn't it feel so good?! As you are vibing higher and higher and higher, and the cells inside you are vibing faster and faster and faster, you will attract other energies in the form of people to take you farther into realms you didn't think possible while still in a body! Again, to use a natural phenomenon, it is like a whirlpool in the middle of an ocean, gathering speed as it draws in other matter.

Michelle met another like-minded girlfriend yesterday, seemingly out of the blue! She saw our book cover online and that Michelle lived near the small town she had just moved to, so she reached out to her on social media. Michelle does not make it a habit to meet up with complete strangers, but she felt a vibrational kinship with this woman, and asked her to meet for coffee.

It was instant "recognition" of a like-minded and like-vibing soul that shared her gender and could relate to her in terms of being female in their shared culture, as well as more spiritual topics. The conversation was easy and engaging, and Michelle felt electrically charged and enthusiastic just being in her company! They had many things in common, from both being writers and intuitive to having similar dogs, and they knew that this was meant to be. How delightful! Michelle's cells are spinning faster as she writes this, as we speak through her, and she gets to relive the experience all over again. So many of you feel that you only find this sort of connection romantically, but there are like-minded others all over the world if you set the intention to meet them; they will gravitate toward you (sometimes instantaneously) when you get the hang of this. (Update: The woman chose to take over Michelle's studio lease for her life coaching business so Michelle could move on to other projects.)

Another example: Michelle is now waiting for the call from the TV producer. Through a series of synchronistic encounters, including her simply writing an affirmation that she is linked to a TV producer who can get her reality show concept to a big network, she met this producer through LinkedIn (notice the same usage of the word "linked") and his last name is even "Powers," like our collective name...

Such signs are not happenstance. In fact, you shall see them become more commonplace as you expand and grow and develop.

Chapter 44

Give Up the Fight

When you "fight the power"—meaning the leaders to whom you give over your collective decisions—all you do is *add power to the fight*. Instead, try tapping into your true innate power and Spirit that creates worlds and entire galaxies! Tap into the interconnected web we all share, and plant seeds of unity, hope, and understanding. Meditate more—and in groups, you are more powerful together—and act out less (including your hateful words on social media) because all you are doing is *adding* to the collective undercurrent of hate, violence, and division. The Truth is *not* that you are separate, as you're often told. The real Truth of you is boundless eternity and infinite Love! When you die, you will know this to be true. You will not be defined by the color of your skin, what genitals you have or don't have, your made-up national boundaries, your religious beliefs—no, you will be included because you are ALL of it—everything! You are pure Light and goodness, and because of that, the good always prevails. Always. So please stop giving your power away! Give up the fight. Doesn't that feel better anyway? Don't be defeated—be the opposite of defeated! Be indefatigable, because that too, is your Truth—the higher Truth of your soul. Tap into *that* Truth now to know peace.

Chapter 45

Harmony Can Be Learned

Just like you take piano lessons or learn any type of instrument, you can learn lessons in co-existence or harmony.

We explained the science of this in our last book, so if you still don't understand, please go back and reread it. In essence, you don't have to all play the same note to achieve a harmonious chord. In fact, you *can't* play the same note and achieve harmony, right? Unless it's an octave off, so you're within a certain range. The point is, you can have differing thoughts and belief systems, but they must all be respected as truth, as part of the higher Truth of us ALL.

And yet, when your thoughts and belief systems affect another negatively—if they are violent and promote separation rather than unity—it will sound like someone pounded the piano. It will not sound melodious—in fact, it will hurt your ears!

You must all come together and *know* you are one for your beliefs to work together. Your creative cultural differences may be woven and intimately intertwined like a quilt. And yet, you too often use them as a cloak or shield.

Your beliefs are not YOU.

This is important, so please pay attention! What if you took your beliefs away? Who are you now?

When you die, you no longer stay attached to your beliefs. Or if you do, you stay stuck in the way station and return to the reincarnation cycle millions of times to learn through suffering and not faith.

We teach the opposite of that—we want you to know that MORE exists! As we've said before, there are literally billions of realities and dimensions beyond this one. Aren't you at least a little curious about them?

We will share with you what our higher existence entails.

My name is Trubien, and Michelle laughed when she heard my name because to her, it sounds like "true being." It could also mean, in French, "very well." I will accept both of those meanings as they are pleasing in your languages.

But I lived centuries before those languages even came into being. In those days, men and women were killed often for basic needs such as food and shelter. We were plagued by disease and famine and feats of nature, hunted by animals.

You—in your "higher societies"—do not face such hardships most of the time. And yet, you still act as if you do.

Together, you could overcome illness simply by using the plants grown all over your planet to give you health—give you life.

You could create shelters for one and all of you, also from materials straight from the earth. *You have everything you could ever need to secure safety, health, and well-being.*

Instead, you still fight like animals. You throw words around like swords and daggers, inflicting emotional wounds as well as physical ones.

Why?

It's time to move forward in peace and understanding. When you feel anger rise, release it in a healthy way—go on a walk or run or move your body in some way to get it out of you, for it is poison. When you disagree with another, simply say so and move on. You do not control anyone but yourself. But when you control yourself, you control all.

Trying to control another is violence in itself. It goes against another's soul agreement and the lessons they wished to learn in this lifetime go-around. Why interfere?

Want to teach someone a lesson? Live it yourself. Be an example. Want to stop another from making laws that hurt others? Step within, shine Light on them, and if you find yourself (physically) directly in front of them, be a shining example of Love and compassion, so that anyone—even those you deem the lowest of the low—may feel your Truth.

We said in the first book that no one likes to be told what to do or say. Do *you*? Communicate that we are One, act like we are One, speak as if we are One—because we are. Others will either catch on, or they won't—and neither is your business.

Keep shining and soon others will gather to your brighter Light. This is contagious, and you have a saying that there is Truth in numbers. So yes, gather together in *solidarity*, but let go of the *fight*, because the fight only begets more anger, fear, resentment, and grief. That's not really what you want, is it?

Be the peace you so desire. Go out in your world, in the small circles of your community, and spread kindness and generosity. Still believe this is passive? Then you are not following our lead, because if you were, you would be seeing the results.

As you see the results of your peaceful existence, share *that*. Share your experiences of kindness, Love, and compassion (please remember the original Latin meaning of "compassion": to love together with). Join hands and hearts, but protest not, for your protests and resistance movements only serve to create movement BACKWARD, not forward...*is that what you want?*

Instead of focusing on what you DON'T want, the source of manifestation is always on what it is you DO want. *What do you want? What do you want right now?*

Chapter 46

All Wars are Caused by a Lack of Focused Light

We have already taught you that beneath it all you are beings of Light and energy. We have shown you how to focus your Light like laser beams on a situation you would like resolved in the highest manner possible, above your own limited belief system. And so, we'd like to point out to you that all acts of violence, terror, and ultimately war between you and another—or between nations—stem from a lack of this focused Light.

You can alter your reality through the use of the Light you already contain. See the Light in you connect with the inner, true Light of another, and already you have amplified *both* of your energies! If the other is your sworn "enemy," know that when you amplify their Light, you amplify your own, for you two are connected. We are all connected, as is everything in the entire Universe.

When you hate another, you hate yourself. When you blame and point fingers at another, you do the same back at you. It is like a boomerang, or a house of mirrors. Stop the blame game, and when you feel that another has done you wrong—or is doing wrong to another group of oppressed people—go within and visualize your Light. See it with a different set of eyes, the eyes of ultimate reality.

You believe your meditations and intentions are somehow passive, that they aren't doing anything at all. Then you go out and complain about your situation with a neighbor or friend or you post on your social media about how bad things are. What is that doing to your energetic offering? If you believe it is doing something positive to go on a rant and protest and resist and complain about how bad things are, you need to go back and reread our other books.

"But we can't just sit around and do nothing! We have to FIGHT!"

That's what we hear you saying. That's what Michelle says when we point out such Truths.

Let's take the recent executive orders of Michelle's United States president. He is acting like a terrorist by building a wall between America and Mexico. He is banning certain Muslims from coming to the U.S. He is taking away the rights of women who fought hard toward progress.

What is the common link there? Walls. President Trump is building walls where there might be bridges.

So let's take this to the individual level. *Where do you have walls built up within yourself?* Where do you still see yourself as "other," and where do you judge other genders, religions, cultures, belief systems?

Please remember, all of those belief systems originated as thoughts in the mind. If they are being reflected in your leaders, simply go back and see where you might own similar thoughts and belief systems in yourself; and then please work to eradicate those limiting, separatist thoughts, for they simply are not real.

The real you is boundless eternity, Love and Light ever in motion. The *real* you doesn't have any walls at all—not toward "others," for in Spirit, it is obvious that there IS no "other." If you feel that you have built up walls toward romantic love and intimacy, ask yourself why. If you are Love incarnate, how do you think you are building up imaginary walls that others can actually feel? Does that feel good?

Probably not. Does building an emotional wall keep you from getting hurt? We would say it does exactly the opposite.

When you build an emotional wall between you and Love, you are sending out the signal of fear that attracts only others who wish to harm you. Again, in the Spirit world where we exist, there is no such thing as fear. Fear belongs to the body, and in this case, to the emotions, which also do not exist where we stand. From our position, we do not need emotional guideposts to where we are "headed," for our destination is "here and now." There is nothing to attain, nothing to aspire to, no one to marry, no job to attain, no fame to be celebrated. It is all Love and Light and Bliss.

You think that is a boring way to be, but that is because you are addicted to drama and suffering. When you can let that go, when you can learn your lessons without suffering and acknowledge their place in your physical lifetime, you are free to be more like us—blissed out and problem free.

When your countries are at war that is not very blissful now, is it? But you can focus your powerful beams of Light and watch what happens. Document the changes. If you can alter peace in your direction in your personal life, imagine what you can do in the infinite field where all things come together?

This president of yours, of America's, is a blessing. He is showing you all how NOT to behave. He is acting out all of your innermost fears, insecurities, and atrocities. Stop the hate in you, and you will affect change in him. Affect change in him, and you affect change in all humanity. If America's president is not your country's president, but you have another leader whom you do not agree with, the same course of action applies. Apply your focused Light to the situation. And then move it outward to countries you do not "belong" to, for you all belong to the human race, don't you? You all chose to come to the planet at this particular time in history to affect change, yes? You all have that much in common, all seven billion of you.

Chapter 47

When a Soul Lesson is Complete

Michelle is asking us what happens when a soul lesson is complete. She must be asking this because she is feeling as if some of hers are "done." There are other teachers who will tell you that you will never get it all "done." We say, maybe not all of it, and certainly not all at once, but you will know a soul lesson is complete by the way it feels. There will simply be no dynamic "charge" to it. The situation will feel more like a story out of a book you read long ago than something that pains you, and you obsess over and re-live the trauma of.

When you "get it," that is, the lesson that you are meant to learn from the repeating challenges and perceived obstacles in your life, just say (aloud if possible), "I get it. I'm done with that, and I now choose to move on."

The Universe will "hear" you (although we have pointed out repeatedly the Universe does not, in fact, have any physical ears), and you will match the higher frequency that vibrates out and forward when you let go of such burdens. That's the way it works.

For example, when Michelle was a teenager, she was violently raped by a man she did not know. This troubled her for some time, and she kept it buried until she felt safe enough to talk about the violence that occurred to her. Fortunately, her therapist not only allowed her to explain what happened to her so long ago, but he allowed her to leave it behind by doing Emotional Freedom Techniques on her that helped her brain release the memory. He helped her see that instead of seeing herself as a victim, she could choose instead to see herself as a valiant survivor!

When she returned to the scene of the rape, she was no longer shaken by the experience. There were no more tears, no more beating herself up, no more rage at her attacker. She simply let it go and was grateful to be alive.

Fast forward to something far less traumatic but currently bothering Michelle at the moment—her inability to calm her nerves on live television. Michelle was on TV early this morning talking about our books and workshops, which she did exceedingly well. Inside, however, she was torn up and experienced a complete lack of sleep the night before. She does not wish to do this to herself anymore. Michelle has been on TV countless times for her own books in the past, and yet her nervousness is still getting the better of her.

Others will tell Michelle that it is something she must encounter forever. And yet, something about that advice doesn't sit well knowing what she does from prior experiences. She does not even know the lesson at the moment, as she is right in the middle of the unpleasant experience. She assumes it is the judgment of others that she fears, and yet she knows, from us, that the "other" is also in her. So that is not it.

We suggest Michelle let it go for now. Allow those feelings of nervousness to rise and witness how it affects her body and mind. In time, she will attract another who might be able to offer healing in this wounded aspect of herself that so many of you also experience. Again, is it not another form of fear? (Update: In the filming of the Australian film/TV show, "The Difference," Michelle realized this fear came from the trauma of being shamed by the hosts on her first television appearance who made fun of yoga, the subject of her first book. The Australian producer then helped heal that past trauma by giving Michelle a heart-opening interview that expressed how she is making a difference on the planet.)

Fears are all illusions. In the same way that you focus your collective Light on wars and other acts of violence, you may shed Light on your fears to make them disappear. It is all an illusion, remember? In the Light of pure presence, all darkness fades away. And fear equates darkness.

Turn on the Light only when you feel ready, when you allow the lesson to surface rather than overrun the mind with analytical evaluations. All that thinking will make your mind burn! Rest in the knowledge that your life is unfolding the way you lined it out for yourself between births, and be excited about what it reveals about you and the inner workings of you.

Chapter 48

The Subsequent Ah-ha Moments

Michelle thought she was finished with our writing session. She was going over this morning's events and she realized that in the midst of facing her fear of speaking live on camera she was truly living her highest life—right there, in that moment!

So many of your lessons come from facing your alleged fears head on and finding that many of them are just false notions of an old self you are leaving behind. Michelle's old self was a victim, and because she no longer chooses to identify with that wounded self, she has more opportunities to change and grow. Sharing our messages with confidence and vigor is at the heart of how she wishes to spend this life! Michelle gets excited at the prospect of full workshops filled with smiling faces and like-minded, like-vibing souls all learning through faith and not suffering. She gets exuberant at the thought of traveling with her soul partner, Jodah, and wandering to various parts of the earth, expounding our messages. Now it is all happening as we said it would. People are growing magnetized to the message, and that message just happens to be coming through her body vehicle.

There will be times along this chosen path that Michelle will have to speak for herself, instead of allowing us to flow through her with words and gestures. She will animate her own body and describe the experience from her personal perspective, and we support her in this process. Our teachings are "spilling over" to her, in the same way we wish your manifestations will overflow into the world.

Our vibrations are syncing up. Did she not know that would happen? She asked for it, but then somehow she didn't believe it could be true, but it is. A part of her must have hidden faith or it would not be aligning. When she lets go of her ego, when she meditates and contemplates nothingness—that is when her vibrational offering rises up to meet ours. Then we are one, just as you all are one.

You, too, may align with us if you wish, and perhaps reach "higher" toward alternate dimensions of reality and teachings that exist. There are many. Find the spiritual master teachers who may lift you up and support you and shed Light on your situations—those places where you are blocking with shadows the Truth of who you really are. It doesn't have to be us. Your spiritual guides could be souls who passed on to the way station before you. It could be souls you've encountered in other lifetimes. It could be what you deem angels, who have never incarnated into a body, and therefore only know peace and harmony. If it feels good, it's not crazy. If alternate realities talk to you of violence and destruction, that is never the Light, and it is not true. Seek a qualified therapist to guide you out of your fears and traumas.

It is your soul purpose to live out your highest and best life while still in the confines of a body! Seek that out for yourself, for it is as individualized as it is creative. For Michelle, being in that moment, and talking about how our teachings have helped her and humanity was a great moment in time (and of course, there is no time). It was a shining soul moment, and if there was one, there can of course be many more.

Michelle was, in effect, afraid of what she most desired. Where is that true for you?

Chapter 49

A Meditation for You

We want you now to get into a comfortable position, breathing in and breathing out, for as long as it takes for you to feel relaxed and somewhat numb.

See yourself as you were before birth, as a streak of Light or perhaps a star or other energy burst! Feel what it feels like to no longer be encumbered by a body, knowing that nothing or no one controls you, and you are free to be boundless and joyous. You are now pure Love, and you might cry if you had eyes with which to tear up, but you don't. And yet, you feel the same feelings as if you were to cry happy tears of joy, only much stronger and more amplified without the body.

You meet up and align with other beams of Light, other starbursts, who match your temperature and rpm. You see how simple this is now! You don't have to try or make anything happen at all. You are it. You are there. You are here. You are everywhere.

In fact, you "see" now that there *is* no "other side," the same as there is indeed no "other" you than you. You are in everyone and are everywhere at once.

How can this be? You don't ask that when you are out of body, for you just know. Bathe in that understanding and wisdom of who you really are and you will never again doubt who you are meant to be.

Stay here a while, without thought, without sound…as if you were in outer space, floating. Stay here a while. Rest and renew. Then return to awareness only when you are ready.

Chapter 50

Finalize the Old Stuff

When your mind continues to travel to any perceived traumas and horrors of the past, try putting an "expiration date" on them.

Memories are transitory unless you continue to bring them up and relive the fearful, low vibrational emotions of them. When you choose to harbor ("keep safe") sad or angry memories, you will eventually make yourself sick, and you will continue to block any positive opportunities, relationships, and adventures that come your way.

In fact, they *can't* come your way by virtue of being on a different frequency. You are choosing to "dial down" your channel and bring yourself lower by bringing forward a memory that is long gone.

Think of it this way: You are watching television and looking for something that interests you in your current mood, or that matches your vibrational set point. You flip through the channels, perhaps spending a few moments watching a program to see if it resonates with what you are wanting, and then you either stay there and watch it to its entirety, or you change the channel.

You may search through your memory banks in the same way. Search for memories that match what you are feeling. It could also be thought of as cleaning out your computer's hard drive. You may find a memory that is sad, and you can watch that emotion for a few minutes to see if it has any merit—any lesson you might still glean from it. Watch it and learn, then change the channel to something more uplifting.

You can make this hard or make it easy. *Who says you must linger in your terrible emotions?* That would be like creating an awful, bitter-tasting stew. Allow yourself to stew in all your positive memories—quiet, loving moments with your loved ones or in nature, memories of traveling to the beach, the mountains, the forest, or wherever you've wandered—thoughts of your existing creations or those still to create: songs, paintings, books, whatever else turns you on.

We want you tuned into the "on" position. ON is Light; OFF is darkness. Turn it off when you rest or go to sleep; otherwise, rise up and energize your life by turning yourself ON. It's much more fun that way—and contagious.

If you find your mind still wants to travel to unpleasant memories, give them an "expiration date." Allow yourself to wallow for a day or so, but never longer than a week, as then your one sad memory could turn into depression or a habit of attracting things you simply do not want.

Finalize the old stuff—the way you were brought up by imperfect parents, the way that ignorant teachers or small children treated you, the lovers or friends or bosses who did you "wrong." All those memories served to push you forward into the expansive state of the ever-moving Universe! They were characters in the "play" of life you created before you were born, so thank them for the opportunity to learn and grow, then release the baggage of the dark emotions you were never meant to carry.

When you die, when you move into the way station and beyond to the places where we reside, you will only harbor feelings of utter peace and joy to have lived the adventure of life and moved through it toward bliss. Remember that, understand the process, and it should be easier to release what no longer serves you. You are better than that. You can choose to now learn through faith and trust and *not* suffering.

You've suffered enough and learned great lessons. Now it's time to learn a different way—through the attraction of everything you've ever wanted, and the giving away of all of it.

Chapter 51

The Original Meaning of Redemption

The word "redemption" has been coming up for Michelle and other teachers of the Light, the way-showers.

When Michelle's sister came to visit, she smelled cigarette smoke often and asked Michelle if it was some spirit trying to tell her something.

Michelle believed it was their uncle who passed several years prior, but she wasn't sure he smoked. When she asked her uncle what he wanted to tell them, she heard the word "redemption."

Michelle's sister said that word sounded like something out of a horror movie. Michelle thought of the word in biblical terms, as in being saved from sin or evil. She looked it up. Another definition is to "regain or gain possession of something in exchange for payment or clearing a debt."

Both women did not know their uncle well when he was alive. Their parents were involved in a lengthy court battle after his death over his estate. So Michelle made it clear to their uncle that they had nothing to do with that court battle, that it was now over and settled, and that he could now let go of these earthly attachments; his soul could be at peace, and he was free to enjoy the wonders of the afterlife.

Fast forward to this weekend's workshop with us. A woman stepped forward to ask us a question, and she said she was an artist on her spiritual path, but that she kept having the same word come up in times of meditation. What was the word? *Redemption.*

When Michelle came home from this momentous event, she looked up the original meaning, which is "the action of buying one's freedom."

We want you to understand something now: you don't have to buy back anything in order to be free. You do not have to be saved from a deity for your alleged "sins," which means your "errors." You all have made mistakes in this lifetime and prior ones, as you were supposed to in order to evolve in a quicker fashion.

Your money doesn't mean anything in the afterworld—in the many billions of dimensions that you could choose to travel to when you die.

We've said this before, and we wish to say it again here now: *You are already free.*

Say it again: "I am already free." "I am free."

Say it until you feel it at the very heart of you.

The word "redemption" is coming up for you because some of you feel as if you are somehow not deserving of such freedom. You erroneously believe that you messed up, made unalterable mistakes, and that somehow you must "suffer for your sins," as many of your religions have taught you.

There is no suffering at all in the afterlife. Any hell fires you've been told exist were told to you by people who mean to control you. When you know that you are already free—no matter what—no one can control you. Isn't that liberating?

When you make mistakes, please know that you were supposed to do so! If you keep making the same ones over and over again, you are only prolonging the suffering. It has become an addiction that you continue to take with you lifetime after lifetime.

But in *this* lifetime, as you have read through all of our books thus far, you were meant to know peace and harmony and understanding. You were meant to remember how free you really are beneath all your society's rules and restrictions. You never "got it wrong," because in the afterlife, *there is no wrong or right*, but only and ever "what is."

Are you starting to get this?

You do not have to "buy back" your soul's purity. It remains eternally untarnished, just like Spirit Source. The more you meditate on this concept, the more it will become ingrained into the heart of you, which never changes. Your heart comes with you into different lifetimes—various scenarios you chose to create a fullness to your soul—and you take your heart with you into the great beyond, into billions of dimensions of bliss; not physically, of course, but your heart is more than just physical, yes?

This brings us to our next lesson.

Chapter 52

Knowing by Heart

What does it mean to you to say you know something by heart? Have you memorized it? Wouldn't you then say you know it by "mind"?

Again, this lesson serves to *re-mind* you that you memorize in the mind during this particular lifetime, and yet, when you know something through and through without even thinking about it, you know it by heart.

Trust that everything you've ever needed to know or will know lies in the heart. It is your connection to the wisdom of hundreds, perhaps millions, of lifetimes—past *and* future. No such thing as time, remember?

When you wish to forgive another or yourself, try placing your hand over your heart and meditate that way. Remember through the heart that you have played countless roles—both "good" and "bad"—throughout centuries of learning. When you see it from a much broader perspective, you know that you were only acting out this role in order to learn and let go, to live a larger, more well-rounded existence that knows compassion *by heart.*

Please affirm this with us now: "I will find new ways to forgive myself so that I can move forward."

The verb form of "redemption" is to "redeem." The first definition that comes up in the dictionary is:

1. compensate for the faults or bad aspects of (something).

synonyms: save, compensate for the defects of, vindicate

We have already established that you do *not* need to compensate for anything, and you do not need to "save" anyone else, for to do so would interfere with their soul's agreement to learn specific lessons through perceived hardships and superimposed obstacles. You yourself do not need saving, either, as we've established that there is zero judgment on the "other side," because there is no true "other side," just varying dimensions that you currently cannot see while in the density of a body. You are already free; you just don't always know it or remember that it is Truth.

If you are free, so is everyone else because you are all connected.

And as far as vindication goes, here are the Google definitions:

1. clear (someone) of blame or suspicion.

2. show or prove to be right, reasonable, or justified.

Again, using our aforementioned understanding of the way things truly are in the Spirit world that lies beyond this current level of reality, do you really need to clear anyone at all of blame or suspicion if they were doing what they did—big picture—to learn what they were made of? You are all here to remember your oneness, and therefore, to "love together with" in compassion toward one another, for you are all made up of Love, and to Love you will all return.

There is no "right" or "wrong." Your actions never need to be justified or reasonable. Those adjectives come from the mind, not the heart.

The heart knows what is "right," as it vibrates at the level of Love, which is the highest frequency there is.

When you live a life of Love, which is your true nature before (physical) life and after death, you would never do harm to another, for doing so would inflict harm upon yourself. When you build walls against another, rather than bridges, you are blocking yourself from all good things. This is not a defensive move as much as an *offensive* one, for it will only serve to keep *you* from evolving to your higher nature.

Someone like Hitler, who performed many offensive acts during his lifetime on earth, is now immersed in Love, his true nature, same as you. He is not being "punished" somewhere, as his soul needed to learn how to be the "bad guy" in a state of harsh contrast in order to propel him forward exponentially so he would not have to return and learn the same old tired suffering lessons time and again.

There is no harsh judge in the sky. You are your harshest judge, and when you see—truly see with new eyes—that this is all in the name of learning, when you affirm you are DONE with your addiction to suffering and complaining and being a victim or oppressor, you will move on through faith to elevated states of be-ing, which will serve to inspire and unite all of humanity.

As we've said, it is time for this now, or we would not be here giving you hints on how to move forward. You've been doing it painstakingly slow, and we are not suggesting you force yourself forward. Quite the opposite, in fact. Nothing happens by force—we said that in our first book. And yet, now that we are well into our third book together, we want you to fly forward as if you were propelled by a sling-shot! Get used to high states of BLISS and renewal, for they are all happening right NOW for you, for ALL of you!

Chapter 53

You Have Outgrown Contrast

Many of you have, that is. If all of you had already outgrown learning through contrast, your world would already be a totality of peace and harmony.

But we know it is not in a state of perfect peace by the violence and strife that is still showing up for you.

But you, *you* are reading this book now. Chances are you have already read our first two books in this series, yes? And of course, there will be many more. If you have not read the other books, that is alright as well, for you found your way toward the vibration of this one, which is at an elevated state.

There are some who have told you that you will ALWAYS experience contrast. You were told that so you would hurry up and learn already! If you knew back then that an experience existed for you without contrast, would you have followed it? You would have pushed for it, fought for it, set a goal, whatever it is you did to make you think you were acting your way toward what it was you wanted, all the while addicted to your suffering and drama as if it were a drug.

You cannot live a full and joyous life of peace and abundance and still feel addicted to suffering and drama. It's impossible.

And yet, we'd like to insert some hope here. You have gotten this far along your path of learning through suffering. When you reach this vista, you might experience some of what you don't want, you might know pain in this bodily existence, but you will now see it with new eyes, and move on rather rapidly. You will rise above the contrast as you let go of fear and resistance—the two go hand and hand and only serve to bring you down with all the "others." Don't go there anymore. It's a decision, and as we said at the start of this lesson, you are more than that. *You have moved beyond.*

Chapter 54

Looking Through New Lenses

Now that you have moved beyond the sea of contrast, you can choose to learn through faith and trust. You simply raise your vibrational offering each day by thinking the thoughts that uplift you and all of humanity. You go forward exponentially *because you know you can*.

Nothing happens until you are ready for it to happen.

That's important. Please read that last sentence again. It doesn't happen because God or the Universe *gives* you something—it is because you have lifted your vibration to a place where good things constantly happen.

When you see things through these new eyes, the world looks more bright and beautiful as a whole. You see the interplay of Light and energy, and it is a spectacular display.

After one of our recent events, Michelle felt so Light and happy and blissful that she looked at her arm and saw a plethora of blue dots all over it, dancing around as brightly as if someone had just flashed a camera in her face.

Those "blue" dots are the true reality. They don't have to be blue, but that color is the vibration Michelle was matching after housing us in her body temporarily. As you know from science, and as we explained in our last book, *Peace is Power*, you have an infinite number of colors that refract as you step into your true reality as a Light being. You are a prism, reflecting Light and therefore various temperatures of heat while your energy is lighting and speeding up! As the rpm's speed up for your cells, inside the very atoms that make up your seemingly solid body, they will heat up, just as Michelle sweats profusely when she is harnessing our energy, which is much faster and, therefore, "hotter."

Your body will adjust to this. You will be drawn toward lighter foods that aren't so heavy, as we've explained previously, and you will want to move your body more because it will be jazzed up and energized. You will need less and less sleep, but be in a state of revitalized wakefulness. This is what happens as you lighten up. It is a most wonderful space to be in!

And it's happening, for some of you. Again, don't worry about the "others." They will catch up, or they won't. It doesn't matter. You are connected to everyone like an old strand of Christmas lights—if one goes out, they all do (except for the newer strings!). As you light up, so do all.

Michelle recently got new glasses. She usually wears contact lenses, but she sees more clearly with the glasses. And so, one day she took her dog out for a walk with the new glasses. Everything seemed brighter and clearer and more beautiful!

Did the things outside change, or was it just her vision that was improved with a simple adjustment?

This segues us right into the next lesson.

Chapter 55

Dark Matter

Michelle and Jodah watched a TV program last night on a science channel that piqued their interest. It was on the subject of "dark matter," and Michelle is asking how this might relate to us from where we stand.

What is dark matter? It's not really "dark," as scientists say it's actually more like "translucent." They can measure its gravity, so the scientists know that it's there. It's just that so far, it's invisible to both the naked eye and their fanciest telescopes.

Does that mean that dark matter does not exist, or that they just can't see it yet, as is the case with Michelle's new glasses, as well as her higher vibratory state?

Michelle Googled that the Universe contains 4.9% ordinary matter (the stuff that you and Michelle can see every day), 26.8 % dark matter, and 68.3% dark energy. So if you do the math, the Universe contains more stuff that you can't yet see than the stuff you currently do.

We don't want to get too far into the science of things, because it is a comical attempt to define what many of you cannot at this point comprehend. Again, the dark matter and dark energy is not "evil," it is simply translucent and invisible, but with a gravitational pull that cannot be explained away.

What if we told you that all this discussion about where we reside and alternate dimensions in time and space, and all the souls who have passed before you and after you—what if all THAT makes up this "dark matter and energy"?

You do not see everything right now. You aren't really supposed to, as it would blow your mind (and body) to pieces! You are immersed in an entry-level existence that wants MORE. That is good because you are getting into the fast and forward moving creative substance of the Universe.

If you can accept that there is far more that you cannot see than that you can see, you are one step closer to actually "seeing" the higher realms.

Acceptance, not resistance, is the way. When you accept, and then immerse yourself in favorable activities with wonderful people around you, cheering you to greatness and supporting your growth, you will see things in a new light. You will see "bodies" as the energetic form they truly are.

This is not just for some, not just for a few sensitive souls who've been born with the ability to see auras and chakras, but for ALL of you to evolve to that place where that is *all you see.*

When you reach this higher plane, you will not ever need an advanced telescope, for that telescope will be YOU! You may reach it in this lifetime, you may reach it in the next, or you may choose, as we have, to move *beyond* into alternate realms where a body is no longer needed—into realms of "dark energy" that is really just CLEAR energy. We'd prefer you use words that more closely resonate with where we are. Your closest vocabulary word to where we reside—where all your divergent choices have taken you into parallel existences and into "heaven" and beyond—is "clear" or "clarity."

Hold the word "clarity" in your mind today as you meditate, and document what you see for the rest of the day. If all you ever requested was clarity, you would reach a place where all things were drawn toward you without even making a request.

Chapter 56

Detachment vs. Disinterest

"When there is no enemy within, the enemy outside cannot hurt you." ~African proverb

Michelle read the above quote on social media and it struck her as something we might wish to discuss in more detail.

We have established that your inner world creates the outer world, always, yes? You are now seeing evidence of this as you practice our tools of shedding Light on situations you have no control over (which is most things).

We have established that you are all connected to a giant web of consciousness, and on a grander scientific external scale, through dark or translucent matter. We have postured that this dark energy is what connects you into various dimensions beyond what you currently comprehend.

And so, we would suggest to you that all the alleged problems you conjure up are pretty small in the overall scheme of things, do you agree? Please go back to the top of this lesson and reread the African proverb. It's a good one.

We offer that when things seem overwhelming to you—as in politics or religion or health or romantic relationships or business/financial matters—the key is to take on an attitude of detachment.

This does not mean you should be disinterested. However, as you learn to "try on" this attitude of non-attachment and witnessing of the events placed before you in this holographic reality, there will be others who see your behavior as "uncaring."

And yet, the exact opposite is true! The more you learn to let go of the energetic baggage that holds you to this existence—which keeps you coming back again and again to lifetimes of learning through suffering—the more you will be trapped in the cycle, and you were never meant to be trapped! You are free, remember?

You let go of this through observed detachment. Remind yourself—talk together in learning groups if you must—that every single occurrence in your world is an opportunity to learn and grow, or for OTHERS to learn and grow.

Watch and learn. Watch and learn. That should be your mantra. When you die—and again, you all will at some point—you will do nothing but watch and learn. You will watch your loved ones with a detached awareness that they are learning their lessons the very best that they can from where they are. You may choose to lovingly guide them through various signs, but not get in the way of their growth and expansion. From this perspective, you will show no emotions other than pure bliss, for there is no reason to harbor emotions. Emotions and feelings are simply guideposts to a better and higher version of your soul. When you die, you ARE the best and highest version of your soul!

Are you understanding the place from which we stand? Even just a little bit? Good. It should make you feel peaceful and at ease knowing you will all go here eventually.

Chapter 57

The Moment of Elation

You have a saying: "When it rains, it pours."

It does not usually mean literally water coming from the sky. Sometimes it means that when "bad" things happen, more unpleasant things happen to follow. It is also analogous to when you have blessings "rain" down upon you, you get much more of the same, yes?

Why do you think that happens?

In the moment of elation, when you are receptive to the bounty you created first in your mind and emotions, you are of an extremely high vibration. Things are clear now. You feel joyous, as if nothing could ever be wrong. Life is good, you feel now, even though it was always in your power for it to be considered "good."

But now that it feels good, and you are relishing in those joyous feelings, you gain momentum and get more of the same, or better! The elation gets stronger and stronger until—you have another saying: you can "hardly contain yourself."

Isn't that interesting? It just might feel as if you are going to explode as your bliss is still housed within the confines of the body. And yet, you can remember that you are more than this body and the unlimitedness of it all will expand.

Or, alternately, you could tell yourself the elation is temporary and short-lived, as nothing ever lasts (another saying, but this one serves to bring your frequency down) and you can effectively get in your own way to sabotage your level of success.

We believe you are past all of that now or you would not be here reading this book. Again, if you have those feelings, it is not "bad," per se. It just means you would do well to read through our first two books and do the tools until you no longer think that way. With no thoughts and clichés and beliefs to put a ceiling cap on your joy, you will continue to rise, and the elation will grow stronger and faster, creating a magnetism that will attract more "good" stuff—again, it could be in the form of opportunities, adventures, relationships, pleasurable objects—you name it, you've got it!

And then, when you learn to maintain a high level of vibration in a semi-consistent manner, you won't even need to name it! You will just travel around, welcoming in activities and experiences that match your level of joy and abundance, and you will maintain a state of utter AWE and AMAZEMENT!

Doesn't that sound better than self-sabotage?

Others will join in on this new higher path, and still others will try to bring you down to their level, but none of that will matter. It will be as if you are in the eye of the hurricane, safe yet powerful, and none of what anyone else does around you means anything at all! It is their path to follow, either with or without you, and you can enjoy yourself immensely while serving as an example of peaceful radiance.

Michelle is currently in this state. Her body is tired, and yet, her mind is light and her spirit a-light! She traveled to meet the TV producer, whom she felt an instant kinship with (because they matched frequencies, of course) and they talked for over two hours about the creative possibilities! It was wondrous, and they amplified each other's enthusiasm and excitement at what lies ahead.

Michelle and Jodah stayed at her college roommate's house nearby, and they met her fiancé who was a former professional comedian turned transformational speaker. As they all talked, Michelle and Jodah saw a perfect example of someone who was highly successful at what it is they wished to do: travel around filling stadiums full of audience members eager to evolve and transcend. It was a perfect match for all of them.

At the end of the evening, when they were all about to go to bed after such a highly exciting day, Michelle checked her email and was told by our publisher that our first book, *Manifesting Miracles and Money: How to Achieve Peace, Purpose, and Plenty Without Getting in Your Own Way*, had hit #1 on the Amazon new hot releases in three different categories!

Michelle was surprised, and yes, elated. We find it amusing that she was surprised, because she has been visualizing our books as bestsellers from the very beginning. She has practiced the feeling of being a bestselling author for many years, even before she allowed us to come through her, so it should come as no surprise. (Update: All of our published books to date have become Amazon #1 bestsellers in various categories, both here in the U.S. and abroad.)

And yet, at the moment of elation, time seemed to stand still. This happens from time to time for you all, yes? Usually in moments of elation or trauma, such as giving birth or getting in a car accident. Because there is no time, it is in those moments of high emotion that you actually FEEL the non-motion and non-existence of time. It is as if you were suspended in space—because in actuality, *you are.*

Now, everyone else went to bed and fell sound asleep. But Michelle was buzzing with excitement, even though she hadn't slept in almost 20 hours. She was careful not to allow those feelings to overwhelm—knowing it's better to savor the delicious feelings in the moment, and then move forward one step at a time, having faith that whatever she needs in the creative process will be delivered. That's how it works, remember?

And so, the next day they spent the morning in their PJs with her old friend, relishing all the pleasant feelings together, not worrying about how it was all going to come together. It was already unfolding as it was supposed to.

Michelle and Jodah flew home, finally got some rest, and had a phone meeting with the producer to reveal that they were "all in." They are ready to step into a bigger life, and when you say a giant YES, the "yesses" line up for you.

Michelle was asked to write a treatment and a storyboard for the show. In the past, as a screenwriter she had learned to do so through a so-called "failed" show that never went anywhere.

You see, *there are no failures*. In learning how to write those necessary "outlines," she now had enough experience to follow through on this new experience that more closely aligned with her highest version of herself.

That too is the way it works.

And so, please revel in your moments of elations. Let them simmer and grow, amplify and ignite and transcend. More will be delivered to you as you do this. We promise.

Chapter 58

Everything is as It Is

Michelle was in her head this morning. She woke up thinking about how on earth she was going to "do it all." In her mind, this meant raise the money needed to achieve all of her aims. After all of our teachings, she still went there, thinking she needs to do everything all by her little egoic self.

The answer to the question that Michelle didn't even know she was asking is that you can't get it all done *on earth* (as in "how on earth?").

You "get" it by understanding that *everything is how it is*. That's the way to let go of the "hows." This may seem like a Zen proverb, but the secret to allowing things to come your way in order to achieve your aims is to aim your way toward acceptance of all things and people—not tolerance, but complete and utter acceptance.

When you do, everything will slide your way.

What Michelle wants, ultimately, is for everyone to want our books. But it's not up to her or us to convince people of anything whatsoever. If someone feels drawn to our books and TV show, it is because they match the frequency of the resonance to a degree that they can allow the information in. That is all.

We've said it before, but we'll say it again here now: you need for nothing. When you truly learn to embrace this, you'll "achieve" a whole new level of freedom—a freedom that was inside of you all along!

Which brings us to our next teaching.

Chapter 59

It's Not Your Fault, but It Is

You are taught in your consumer-based societies that you lack something so that someone else can sell it to you in order to make you feel complete.

We want to tell you again and again that you lack for nothing, and you are already whole and complete exactly as you are. You need for nothing.

If you want something, that is okay, and if you follow our suggestions, you'll likely find yourself with it or living it out. And yet, you don't need this book either.

All the answers lie within you. You know this, and yet you put your trust in others' hands.

There is a very famous manifestation writer with a big contract at a big publishing house who, in her marketing, will tell you that the only reason you haven't gotten what you wanted is because you believed that it was just a matter of your belief system not being enough, and that it just isn't your fault.

In order to remedy this, you need her new book and videos.

We are not going to agree with that sentiment, as it is without integrity. Yes, there have been millions of dollars made from you believing things aren't your fault, and the word "fault" itself implies blame, judgment, and doubt, which are extremely negative connotations.

But please pay attention here: If nothing is your fault, there is nothing within your power to change.

We are here to empower you to know you can change anything and everything or nothing. It is all within you. It is all an inside job. You don't need this book at all! You may want it, you may love reading it, you may hate it, and none of this matters except the meaning you bring to it.

We aren't here to "sell" you our ideas. We are here to remind you of the power you contain within you to change your world. *Your* world, not anyone else's. Change *you*, and you radiate positivity and hope to others. That "radiation" will do more for humanity's overall vibration than anything we can do or say from our non-physical perspective.

So why not "take it on"? The ownership, that is, of your own life story. After all, you wrote the script in between lives. You are the editor in chief! You are the producer, the director, the entire cast. YOU.

So we're *not* going to point out the obvious and say "take responsibility" for it because that is another low-vibing word of yours. Responsibility is the opposite of play, and we sincerely hope you play more, not less. We sincerely hope you don't take this all so seriously.

We just want to point out that if nothing is ever your fault, then you have no power. And people will try to sell you stuff you think you need to make you whole.

We'll say it one more time for emphasis: YOU ARE ALREADY WHOLE!

Now, if you WANT to buy their stuff because you believe it will offer you a pleasurable experience and you resonate with whatever is being offered that is a different matter entirely. We hope that is exactly what you are feeling as you read our words each day. As we keep repeating, as you feel these pleasurable emotions, your vibrational offering lifts and you are more apt to bring all things and experiences and people and adventures and opportunities toward you.

But you certainly don't "need" to. And yes, you do have the power already. It is yours, which makes it your "fault." We wish you had a different word with a more positive connotation than "fault."

Think about it. What's another definition for "fault"? It's the crack in various places of your earth caused by—and the cause of—earthquakes. It's either a rift in the dirt or implied criticism.

Don't fall into the "rift" by thinking you need for something or someone. It's simply a "hole" where there is none.

Instead, come from a place that knows no rifts or criticism of any kind, and you'll reach new levels of bliss that have nothing to do at all with your material manifestations.

Chapter 60

Money and the Lack Thereof

Michelle was feeling happiness and fulfillment from the many reviewers who gave their positive judgment and opinions of our first book, *Manifesting Miracles and Money*.

Of course, we'd like to point out how silly it is to feel a certain way over the basis of someone else's opinion, but because it was "good," she felt happy.

Of course, when you base your happiness or unhappiness on another's point of view, when it is unfavorable, the opposite is true. You might feel sad, angry, or disappointed, among other low-vibrational emotions.

Neither is the Truth of who you are.

And yet, you base your self-worth on this. We don't "care" at all what others think of our words, they are just guideposts to the Truth of us anyhow. They are not the Truth itself, just "arrows" to get "there," which is really where you stand right now.

Have we confused you yet?

The reason for this lesson is that Michelle was surprised to see a few reviewers turn down the opportunity to share their opinions with the world because they did not believe in "money."

We find this notion hysterical, yet Michelle was confused. How could someone hate money? Money can do much good for so many, as long as it's viewed as its original source, which is simply an exchange of goods and services, Michelle thought.

We'd like to further this line of thinking by pointing out that money, like anything else, is just energy.

Many of your teachers have taught you this, and yet you still do not act as if this is the case. We appreciate you using the terms abundance and plenty and wealth, as those terms embrace the fullness of having other sorts of prosperity rather than just paper or metal money, which is exchanged for goods and services.

Focus on the goods and services themselves, and you've done away with the need for money.

That's important. Please read it again. We asked Michelle to highlight it for you all. When you reject money, you are saying you don't wish to have goods and services. You can get goods and services in millions of ways if you are creative and have learned to project your vibration in such a way that it attracts every "need" you think you could ever have.

And yet, of course, as we've said in prior books, if you hoard it all to yourself it is as if you create an energetic blockage that will eventually create dis-ease or other such maladies. Through The Law of Circulation—and it's not really a law as much as a natural state of organic movement—what you give out you receive, in a multitude of ways and in bountiful measures!

If you think money is "evil"—please ask yourself your definition of evil. We've pointed out before that the word "evil" was just another way of saying "bad" until the 1800s. After that, the word took on a supernatural force that it just doesn't have.

And money isn't "bad" either. There is no bad or good, remember? Only your perception and judgment makes it so!

Money combined with your own innate state of freedom amplifies the good it can do in the world.

When you give and give and give some more, you will live in a harmonious state of existence. At least try this! Try this exercise before you label it as a "bad" one.

If you don't want money, indeed you'll never get any. And if you don't get any, then what will you do to aid in your growth and that of another? Without money, will you give of yourself in service? In what ways? Please take some time to write out how you could use your money in positive ways so that all may thrive. When all thrive, your world will know peace.

That does not sound all that bad, now does it?

Chapter 61

You Don't Have Anything to Do Today

Michelle woke up feeling like her "to-do" list was a mile long. She did not want to get out of bed; her sense of obligation and responsibility felt overwhelming.

And so, she did just a little bit of yoga to stretch her body, clear her mind, and get centered. In the present moment, the "to-do" list just doesn't exist.

Have you ever felt overwhelmed with responsibilities? Whether you feel tethered to a job, your children, your parents or friends, it doesn't matter. It just doesn't have to get done today.

In the midst of Michelle creating her list last night, she intuited her eldest daughter was in trouble. It turns out that the Oroville dam was expected to burst from the recent heavy rains, and her daughter was directly above it! She had gone to visit her grandparents and was on her way home when officials called the evacuation.

Suddenly, Michelle's "list" of responsibilities stopped. She began to worry, and then, she stopped herself, knowing that her worry would simply project fear onto her daughter's path, which is exactly what she did not want to happen.

And so, she stopped everything and went to lie down on her bed. She pictured pouring golden Light all over her daughter, her daughter's new car, the Oroville dam, the lake, the people living in Oroville, and those who've been evacuated to shelters and who were on the packed roads trying to escape.

She poured Light until she began to feel a little better, and then her daughter texted her that she was still on the roads, but she was okay. Her daughter had bought a stranger a sandwich at the gas station because she didn't have any money. Her daughter, even in an apparent emergency, still demonstrated an act of kindness.

All you ever need "do" is be kind.

Please remember this when you feel overwhelmed by meaningless tasks. They will get done in the right order. When survival comes first, everything else falls away. When people are at the end of their lives, things go undone, and life still goes on for others.

Simply do something that brings your awareness into the present moment, such as yoga or a walk or reading a book (maybe even this one!), and then go forward one "task" at a time, starting with the ones that most excite you, not the ones you dread.

Coming from a sense of dread will only bring you to a lower vibration, rendering you unable to complete the rest of what you wish to accomplish! Sometimes, people try to do those dreaded things first in order to "get it over with." And then, by the time the first task is complete, they have no energy to do anything else.

Find something that gets your heart pumping first! THEN follow through with one thing at a time, and before long, you will find you're almost there. And if you don't get it all done? Again, your mission on earth is not to get it all done. You will NEVER get it ALL done...even when you pass on to other realms you won't have all your "missions accomplished," but you won't care a bit.

Simply be. Do things out of that sense of being-ness where time stands still and words and actions flow like rivers.

Chapter 62

Believe it Into Being

Nothing happens if you don't believe in it.

This may sound rudimentary, and yet, we see how often you want to make something happen with your words and in your head, but your energy tells another story.

Others schooled in the "Laws of Attraction" will have you focus on your "blocks" to your desires. But we advise that is about the worst thing you can do if you want to move forward.

If something is not happening to you or for you in a favorable fashion, it is always and ever about your frequency match to it. We've told you this before, but thought we'd say it again in a different fashion so you really hear it.

If you are not of the same frequency as your desire, it is always only and ever about your "doubt." And if you focus on doubt as a block to your joy, you will become more blocked.

Instead, try asking yourself why not you? Why should you not have all that you desire? It all comes back to doubt—doubt that you are not good enough, attractive enough, smart enough, *enough*.

Instead of questioning your blocks and the emotions behind them, tell yourself you are enough until you feel it. When you feel so-so, say (aloud if possible), "I am enough. Of course I am enough. I am more than enough, as are we all."

When doubt creeps in, it can also be about the "how," how is it going to happen, and your mind begins its analyzing and scheming instead of allowing and flowing.

Simply observe your mind and ego doing its thing, and quickly change direction. Feel the wondrous feelings of joy and bliss that are at the heart of you, which we describe over and over again, that *attainment of anything* at all is ever and only a glimpse to the greater expansive part of you.

Again, once you die and enter the space between lifetimes and beyond, you will know all of your desires instantaneously! Imagine that now, please. Imagine all your desires attained NOW. Those are the feelings more closely associated with where we are. We are beyond all the longing, but you will never get here until you can match the emotions equated beyond desire.

Sure, you're probably going to keep wanting things while in a human state of existence. It's part of the package. And yet—and this is the part we want to get you to—you can *want things for another* to skyrocket your peace! Better—turn their "want" into a "thing or experience" by your amazing manifestation skills and higher resonance! Now, instead of just gathering stuff that gives you pleasure, instead of checking things off of your bucket lists, you have an entire planet for which to give hope and with whom to share your gift of promise and plenty.

This is exciting to us! This is a world we might consider coming back to if we weren't already so blissed out in the afterworld.

Michelle and Jodah are following through on their dreams. The TV show is in progress, and Michelle watched as feelings of doubt crept into her consciousness. Just as quickly, she reminded herself of the true purpose of the show: NOT to become a famous celebrity; that is not really her style, but MORE about elevating the consciousness of many through the spread of our teachings—through our books and workshops and online channeled coaching programs—on a grand scale.

It is already happening as she focuses on the real reason for the show. Without the show completed, our books are becoming international bestsellers and events and online programs are selling out. More invitations to speak are coming in from all over, and sponsors are requesting to be a part of it. It's all happening, and yet, if Michelle or Jodah continued to focus on their "doubt," on any perceived feelings of being not good enough or afraid of judgment or exposure or being a "celebrity," they would vibrate at a lower level not conducive to the grand expansion of our word that they seek.

We want it, too. And yet, again, we are beyond wanting. We see it as already happening, because on other "channels" of time and space—what you deem "alternate dimensions," it is. Tap into that, as we have suggested before, and you bring yourself to the "highest" and best place you can be.

Chapter 63

Wanting Rain and The Law of Propulsion

Michelle woke up to heavy rains on her house—again. It's been pouring buckets for weeks now in Northern California where she resides, and her first thought as she got out of bed was how much she'd like to be in the sun somewhere at the moment.

The rain should come as no surprise. While it's been considered a drought for the last few years in her state, and the fear mongers in the news predicted nothing but doom and gloom for its inhabitants, the people of California said to each other—almost daily—that "we NEED the rain."

Every single time it so much as sprinkled, Michelle heard someone tell another person how great it was that it was raining, for we all *need* it so much.

Michelle just figured the earth would adapt, as it always does, and that as the inhabitants of the earth, we too could adapt (adapt does mean "change," and as we've said numerous times, you are always changing and growing whether you want to or not).

And yet, as the people of California focused their collective thoughts and beliefs on the desire for rain, in 2017 it came down in droves, so much so that it became quite destructive in many areas, almost breaking dams, causing traffic problems, and flooding roadways and homes.

Then the people of California scratched their heads and the fear mongers put up "Storm Watch" footage on the news of all the destruction, and *now* they want it to stop.

How we view this from our non-physical perspective is this: your collective focus built up a tremendous momentum energetically that—like a dam—burst open when the time was right. It will take some time to slow down the momentum of the last several years—it is like a whirlpool of energy in what Abraham would call the "vortex," and we might call space.

This phenomenon is completely understandable through the lens of The Law of Attraction, yes? Now you can understand the sheer FORCE of energy propelled forward as so many wished for the same thing at once, in droves, for long periods of time! Through The "Law" of Propulsion—and we would call it more of a Truth than a Law—your collective "wants" became a skyrocketed reality!

In time, the rains will subside, as they always do. The people of California, for the most part, are still learning from contrast, and so they will build new and bigger dams, and they will fix the roads and clear the debris from falling branches.

And yet, there is an important lesson here to learn from the rampant rains. What if you put that much thought and feeling into your own wants? You might still have them at this point, yes? Abundance, health, wealth, relationships, travel, adventure?

Better yet, what if you put your thoughts and focus on PEACE, the focus of our teachings to you?

What if, instead of saying to one another, "We need more rain," you said, "We need more peace"?

From there, you see, you could turn your need into a "want," which is less desperate. "We want more peace."

From there, you could take it to the next level: "Let's have or enjoy more peace."

In order to enjoy peace on a collective level, first you must see it internally, as we keep saying. And so, please ask yourself now, are you enjoying peace in this moment? If not, why not? What inspired actions might you take in order to enjoy a life of peace and serenity and harmony?

If relationships in your life are not harmonious and peaceful, what might you do to change that? Have a "peace talk" with any persons in your life you feel are an impediment to your peace, and if that communication fails because of differences in vibrational frequency, please gravitate toward others that may share your sense of peace. In that way, peace is amplified!

If your finances and/or health are what's keeping you from enjoying peace, please take some time today to feel grateful for whatever money and health you *do* have at the moment, and in that focus it will grow; it will eventually "rain" down on you—in droves, if enough harmonious others share your vision of peace!

Do you see where we're going with this?

The word "drought," like all your words, has several meanings:

> 1. a prolonged period of abnormally low rainfall; a shortage of water resulting from this.
>
> *synonyms*: dry spell, lack of rain, shortage of water
>
> 2. a prolonged absence of something specified.
>
> *archaic* thirst.

We have discussed the first definition of drought—as in California's former rain shortage. But isn't it interesting how it also means "a prolonged absence of something specified."

What is the prolonged absence of something specified in your individual life?

The original definition meant "thirst."

And so, we'd like to ask the question: what it is you still thirst for?

Please focus your laser-like feelings of Light upon whatever is in the "gap" for you now, so that it may spill out for others. Please fill yourself to the brim with whatever lights you up, so that you may be a Light unto the world! Please turn your focus, then, from things and needs and wants to the bigger picture of peace for humanity, so that you ALL may finally rise up and unite, for that is at the root of all your needs and wants anyway.

Chapter 64

Raining Creative Opportunities

As Michelle and Jodah have focused their desires upon more creative opportunities in which to spread our messages, more have rained down upon them, as in our last example.

Michelle was writing and stating (to herself) that she was a bestselling author before she actually became one! She drafted an outline of her TV show before she met a producer who captured her vision and helped make it a reality.

Now, Michelle is feeling as if she is struggling to juggle all the creative opportunities she put into her "spacial bank of desires," and so, we are suggesting to her that she simply see it all as done with ease and flow—like a nice, easy rainfall instead of a downpour.

You can alter your vision at any time! It may take a little bit for your new offering to catch up with the sheer volume of your former desire, but it can be altered all the same. When you are feeling overwhelmed by the abundance of your manifestations (and yes, it *can* happen we assure you!) then take a step back and see it as all done in perfect timing, at a pace that feels good to you.

It can be as if you are "dialing down" the knob of time on your computer. If you want to dial it up and speed up the manifestation of your want, then do so! Use your imagination as we have taught you in our previous two books. If you want to slow things down, even incrementally, you have the power to do this in the exact same way.

Please remember how truly powerful you are…

We'd like to go over again how once you have the hang of manifesting for yourself, what a joy it becomes to join in on the manifestations with others.

You are all one. When you lend your Light force energy with another, you also do this for yourself. It is easier for you to see the vision of another without "bringing it down" by the thought of "needing" it. You need for nothing, remember?

Practice seeing a dream coming true for a friend or family member now. Take a few moments in meditation to imagine the joy they'll have at receiving their want. Feel that joy and fulfillment now deep inside yourself. Know that their joy is also your joy!

Michelle and Jodah's current dream is to have our TV show, *Don't Change the Channel*, funded and to start filming. To help seed the project, they are selling the RV they were given by a former client.

Originally, the dream was to use the RV to travel to our events. And yet, as you well know, dreams often *change*. Their schedules got full, and they realized they preferred staying at the hotels we speak at, and so, selling the RV to recoup the money put into it to run efficiently seemed like the right thing to do.

While there was a lot of interest in the RV, there was one woman in particular who wrote to Michelle about how excited she was to get this RV. She told her how when she was younger and a "hippie," she travelled around the country to various festivals and felt so free and happy! This woman wanted to do this now in her later years to feel that same sense of freedom and happiness.

This woman has not even purchased the RV yet, but while reading her letter, Michelle felt that same sense of freedom with her.

When the woman buys the RV, it will help fund Michelle and Jodah's dream. At the same time, it will fulfill the different dreams of a complete stranger. At the heart of both "dreams" is the desire for freedom, which all of them—and all of you—already contain. As you feel your innate sense of freedom more and more, reminding each other how it truly feels, the more examples of freedom you will manifest with and for one another.

That's the way it works.

Chapter 65

Opposing Without Hatred

Michelle was watching the Academy Awards show last night on television.

There was one acceptance speech that stood out to her, when someone said we could oppose something without hatred.

When you stand in opposition to something, it is just the contrast that you might need to propel you forward. And yet, if you add to that feelings of hatred—defined as intense dislike or enmity, you are keeping yourself in a frozen low-vibrating state that will attract everything you oppose TOWARD you…

You may find it interesting that the original Old English word for hatred was: "to advise, discuss, rule, read, guess." So to hate something originally meant to try to work it out…

Of course, the antonyms for hatred are love and attraction.

Which would you rather be a part of?

Allow opposition to propel you and humanity forward, and everyone wins.

Keep yourself stuck in a cycle of enmity and you—and everyone else connected to you, which is EVERYONE—loses.

Where can you use the original meaning of hatred to find common ground? You may not agree with another's opinions, but that is not the Truth of who they are. That's just a thought they obsessed on over and over again until it became their version of reality. What's YOUR version of reality?

Michelle read a post this morning from a man she usually agrees with and whose words she finds uplifting.

But this time he was promoting "hard work," which Michelle finds distasteful. She thought, "Why would you engage in society's version of hard work if you can imagine the feelings of having the goal and allow it to manifest effortlessly?"

Perhaps the difference lies simply in their apparently divergent definitions of "hard work" versus ease, you see. For some, engaging in "hard work" is an enjoyable task they don't wish to give up. For Michelle, the word "effort" aligns more closely to what she gives out when she writes our books with us. It does not feel "hard" to her, as she is excited and engaged with the outflow.

Again, there is no right or wrong here, neither good nor bad. It's simply your perception of things that is skewed by your historical viewpoint of life experience.

CHAPTER 66

All Movements are Toward Acceptance

What do the following words have in common: persist, resist, dissidence, activist?

You may be thinking they are all words that denote opposition to a belief system, and you would be right. And yet, we'd like to point out how each word contains within it the verb "is."

Why is this important? We see, from our nonphysical perspective, that ALL of your movements are toward acceptance.

Please think about this. The Civil Rights Movement, Women's Rights, LGBTQ Rights, the list goes on and on…

At your core, all of you are exactly the same. When you die, you will lay witness to this very basic fact. Without skin, national borders, or genitals—without a bank account or house or anything else to identify you as ego—you are Spirit. You know this by now, don't you?

And so, we encourage you to use the word "movement" when you gather together to encourage evolution among people toward acceptance. What you resist persists, as we keep pointing out...So that's no good. If you can retain your optimism as an activist, then you will assist in moving things forward. If you can adopt a calm demeanor in the face of judgment or defamation, you win, and everyone wins.

Chapter 67

Miscommunications and Misunderstandings

Michelle accepted a new yoga job last month because she claims she has no self-discipline to keep doing her yoga regularly unless she is working; and the yoga feels good for her body and mind.

But now her frequency is far ahead of where she was when she began learning and teaching yoga decades ago. And so, because of this energetic differential, she began seeing problems and challenges with this job and interacting with others, so last night she quit.

We create our own obstacles by our resistance to forward-growing motion and change. It is not the yoga that is "bad," it just doesn't fit where Michelle is going and the direction we are all moving.

It began with a miscommunication stemming from ego. Michelle substitute-taught for another teacher who confronted her in front of other members about "taking over" her class, when it was *she* who showed up on the wrong day. Rather than creating a problem, Michelle pointed out that she was there to help when teachers needed a day off for whatever reason, but because of the mistake, she would simply work out while she was there and then go home.

Then it happened again.

When misunderstandings happen more than once, it now becomes a decision going forward. And there are definitely atmospheres of misunderstandings, based on who is at the top of a business making the hiring decisions of those in their midst (like attracts like vibrations).

Yet Michelle ignored this and went ahead and accepted employment when the previous teacher left permanently. Now that that person was gone, another lower vibrational person simply took her place. The accountant did not introduce herself, but said Michelle needed to fill out employee paperwork that had already been turned in.

Rather than get involved in unnecessary conflict, Michelle turned in the paperwork she was asked to. The accountant kept saying it wasn't there when it was. Michelle was confused, so she came in to clarify with another manager.

It turns out that if the accountant had simply stated the subbing paperwork she had as an independent contractor wasn't the same as that needed to become an employee, all would have been cleared up!

Your words and language form an incomplete energetic translation, you see. But if used properly, they have the power to promote kindness and unity.

When someone's words continually are rude and hurtful, first try to provide clarity for a solution, but if someone stubbornly stays in a position of opposition, see it for what it is, please: an energetic frequency difference.

How do you know this is true? By the way it feels. Michelle felt sick all day because of the way this accountant, whom she never met in person, was treating her through emails. And so, she put an end to it and effectively "pulled the plug" from this downward-spiraling interchange.

How does this minor misunderstanding affect you?

Where do you find you stay mired in situations that do not best support you based on what other people say and how you "should" feel? Do you tell yourself you "must"? Because we have established now that you "need" for nothing. Therefore, you "must" not do anything that does not align with your soul and Source energy. Only *you* know where that vibrational offering is currently set, but if you want it to go "up" instead of "down," you will do well to be in an environment of peace and harmony with people who know how to use their words toward kindness, not strife and drama.

Whether this is in your work relationships, romantic partnerships, or friendships does not matter. Again, what you stand for personally is what you will see on a much grander scale as a hologram for your world! When your "leaders" (whom you put in charge of you) cannot agree and communicate with leaders from other countries, the same sorts of misunderstandings occur. "Unplug" from their energy, and see them drenched in golden Light the same way you would do for your individual experiences. See the leaders of your world representing the values you follow on a personal level—honesty, integrity, courage, peace, love. If you cannot radiate such feelings in the midst of conflict, how can you expect them to?

This always goes back to the Truth that we are all connected, all one. When a part of the whole of Spirit is out of alignment, and they do not respond to your energetic offering, let them go find their own.

You are beyond all this.

Chapter 68

Abundance is Expansion in Motion

We have established in our past books how the cells in the body and in the planets in your Universe are in perpetual motion and circulation. The Universe is always moving forward in a state of ever-evolving creation. When you are a part of this flow forward, you feel fantastic, because you are moving *with* the natural order of things. And yet, when you fear change and transformation and stay stuck in resistance, you will not feel that great. You've likely experienced this by now, yes?

Once again we'd like to point out that your level of abundance—and by this word we do not mean only money—is simply a part of expansion.

When you are not expanding with the organic, positive flow of the Universe, your level of abundance will reflect this. Abundance is how much goodness your life can contain: joy, health, wealth, relationships, adventure, new experiences, artistic endeavors…and the list goes on.

When your bank account balance is low, when you are tired and run down and ill, when "mean people" seem to be all around you and out to "get" you, it simply means you are running low in abundance, like a gas tank runs low in gas.

How do you fill it? By focusing on the "gas" you do have! You may see evidence of low funds, but you must have some or you wouldn't be able to buy this book. You may not feel vibrantly healthy and energetic, but you are still alive or you wouldn't be reading this book. You may be experiencing low-vibrational people because you haven't found the courage to "unplug" and find new friends and associates who lift you up and inspire you to new heights!

All this is changeable, you see. Focus on the good, and the good expands. Not only does it expand, but it does so rapidly because it is the natural order of things. You know that saying, "going with the flow?" That's a true statement, as you are always going with or against the flow of energy. Which do you choose right now?

Chapter 69

You Don't Have to Convince Anyone of Anything

Yesterday Michelle was having coffee with a new friend. She was thrilled to match vibes with another female, and so she was looking forward to this day. But when she went inside the coffee shop to order, directly behind her sat a group of three older men who spoke their opinions loudly.

Their racial slurs seemed to echo in the quiet coffee house, and Michelle found her blood pressure rising and her heart beating louder in anger at their offensive words. She almost turned around to give them a "dirty look" or even confront their hostility with more hostility, and then she realized doing so would only add "fuel to the fire," as you often say, and her getting angry would not change their minds anyway.

And so, internally she said "rise" until she felt better. She went outside and spent several hours in glorious conversation with another like-minded soul, and the old men left the building.

When Michelle was about to go home, she stopped by a jewelry store across the street. It was the same store where Michelle had replaced her watch battery last time, but the new battery only lasted a month. She explained this to the clerk, who started to say that the man who replaced batteries was out of town, then she took a call. It was a personal call, and the woman proceeded to ignore Michelle and go in the back room for a loud political argument with her "friend."

Michelle put her watch back on, and the watch started to work again! It had been dead for more than a month! So she laughed and left the store while the angry woman was still on the phone in her heated discussion.

Michelle relayed this very story on social media. Many laughed with her. Some said more angry things, like she should have reported the matter. Michelle thought the "moral" of the story was to create better boundaries when people treat you poorly, or that there is no such thing as time, as we keep teaching her.

And yet, we'd like to explore more of what happened here.

Michelle was getting irritated by the offensive political talk of the three men in the coffee shop. At the moment of annoyance, she stopped the momentum of her outrage understanding that it would only add to the undercurrent of rage in the atmosphere. Instead, she proceeded to lift her vibration through the use of the word "rise" and the uplifting shared conversation with her friend. As they sat outside in the beautiful sunshine, they attracted other friends from the community to hug and laugh together with.

She then encountered a new situation with yet another angry person. But this time, Michelle's vibration was at a higher level where she didn't take it as a personal affront. Knowing that you cannot truly convince anyone of anything ever, she put her watch back on and her new energetic offering "jump-started" the watch.

You're all energy, remember? Why couldn't this happen?

Then, feeling empowered, Michelle simply left the negative situation, effectively "unplugging" from the lower-vibing woman, and went home happy with her watch still working.

We will say this again: You cannot convince anyone of anything, ever.

Live out your life story the best you can, and teach by example. Set your boundaries by walking away, and as the great master teacher Jesus said, "Turn the other cheek." This is *not* passive; it's attaining energetic harmony that is stronger than your shared animosity with another.

Have you ever heard, "Don't sink to their level?" We agree, don't "sink." Rise up together, and know peace. Those who don't share your beliefs have their own soul agreements to honor and lessons to learn. If you feel moved to communicate your position on something, do so in a state of calm assurance, and walk away if it is not well received.

Chapter 70

Violence = Ignorance + Resistance Amplified

So what do you do when someone else erupts in violence?

We'd like you to understand the source of violence before you react. Violence is a simple equation. It is ignorance plus resistance, amplified.

What does that mean? First, what is the definition of "ignorance?"

1. lack of knowledge or information.

synonyms: incomprehension of, unawareness of, unconsciousness of, unfamiliarity with, inexperience with, lack of knowledge about, lack of information about, lack of education, unenlightenment, illiteracy, lack of intelligence, stupidity, foolishness, idiocy; *informal* cluelessness about

From here, what is the definition of "resistance?" We've shared the first definition previously. We'd like to explore the *second* definition.

1. the refusal to accept or comply with something; the attempt to prevent something by action or argument.

synonyms: opposition to, hostility to, refusal to accept

2. the ability not to be affected by something, especially adversely.

This SECOND definition of resistance is the one we encourage you to use more often, as in raising your vibration so high through the habit of doing things and activities that are pleasurable for ourselves and our unique souls, that NOTHING affects us—not even other people's *resistance*, as in the *first* definition which equates hostility.

When you put together the feelings of "not knowing any better" with "hostility," and then you AMPLIFY those emotions, what erupts is often the physicality of thought and feelings into form. In other words, violence.

There are violent manifestations in the same way there are positive manifestations, you see? It is all just thoughts, beliefs, and feelings into form.

And so, the question becomes, what do you want to amplify?

Again, let's explore your Google definitions of amplify, including the fascinating original meaning:

1. increase the volume of (sound), especially using an amplifier.

synonyms: make louder, louden, turn up, magnify, intensify, increase, boost, step up, raise

2. increase the amplitude of (an electrical signal or other oscillation).

3. cause to become more marked or intense.

Origin: late Middle English (in the general sense 'increase, augment'): from Old French *amplifier*, from Latin *amplificare*, from *amplus* 'large, **abundant**.'

So what do you want to amplify—to increase, magnify, make ABUNDANT?!

Do you wish to increase hostility and violence on your planet, or do you want to be a part of peace and equanimity? Raise your vibration daily and see how it feels for you. Raise your vibration when you are feeling triggered by what another has to say. Raise your vibration when you are already feeling "on top of the world" and amplify THAT higher emotion, a place where nothing and no one can bring you "down."

Chapter 71

The Opposite Equation

From here, because we are starting to understand what creates violence, let's now explore how to create the opposite of violence, which is peace, and to amplify more peace.

If Violence = Ignorance + Resistance Amplified, **Peace = Wisdom + Unity Amplified**

Again, let's break it down in your own man-made forms.

noun: **wisdom**

> 1. the quality of having experience, knowledge, and good judgment; the quality of being wise.
>
> *synonyms:* sagacity, intelligence, sense, common sense, shrewdness, astuteness, smartness, judiciousness, judgment, prudence, circumspection; logic, rationale, rationality, soundness, advisability
>
> 2. the soundness of an action or decision with regard to the application of experience, knowledge, and good judgment.

3. the body of knowledge and principles that develops within a specified society or period.

synonyms: knowledge, learning, erudition, sophistication, scholarship, philosophy; lore

And unity:

1. the state of being united or joined as a whole.

synonyms: union, unification, integration, amalgamation; coalition, federation, confederation

2. the state of forming a complete and pleasing whole, especially in an artistic context.

synonyms: harmony, accord, cooperation, collaboration, agreement, consensus, solidarity; *formal* concord, concordance

3. a thing forming a complex whole.

synonyms: oneness, singleness, wholeness, uniformity, homogeneity

Origin: Middle English: from Old French *unite*, from Latin *unitas*, from *unus* 'one.'

So let's put this all together. When you connect knowledge, experience, common sense, and learning with harmony, cooperation, accord, and collaboration, you create peace. When you feel peace, you amplify—or magnify and intensify—peace, which begets more peace, which is part of the organic forward-flowing force that drives the entire Universe.

CHAPTER 72

The Less I Personify God and the Universe, the More Empowered I Become

When you call God a "he" or even a "she"—as if this glorious force for good could have a body with skin and genitals and limited perception—you limit your own power to create something from nothing.

You are all God, and God is in all of you. You are all Love, and the force of Love runs through and around all of you! You are indeed a speck of the fullness of the entire Universe, and thus, the ENTIRE UNIVERSE runs through the very cells and atoms of your body and soul...isn't that exciting?

When you label something so BIG and bountiful, you lessen its potential for more and better. We are here to tell you that you simply cannot contain the immensity of your innate power while you are still experiencing and experimenting inside of a body. You can catch glimpses and KNOW and TRUST that the flow exists, but the only way to truly feel the God within is to let go of your imperfect images and labels and just let it be.

The more trouble you have with this notion, the more you are attached to your old thoughts and belief systems, you see. The more attached you are, the more you will reincarnate into this existence until your inner vision expands beyond this current reality. Release your baggage and look for more and better—not in things, per se, you're beyond that now—but to more and better for all humans everywhere…actually, for all be-ings, for we're not all human exactly like you.

Again, there are literally billions of dimensions ABOVE and BELOW this current one where you create your own reality. Don't limit yourself to one almighty deity who controls your life and who you can order around and beg for things to be different than how they are. Surrender, yes, as in allow the process to unfold as you maintain a high energetic frequency, but not to any one "person" or "leader." You have free will! It's a true gift that you all asked for—all 7+ billion of you! You all have that in common, this aligned movement of free will and making matter from original thought. Focus on your commonalities and you will discover unity in all things. Focus on the perceived separation of religions, polities, and various ideologies, and you will know only strife. Strife will destroy all that you have built together.

Try this: What would happen if you believed without a doubt that everything always works out for you, no matter how it looks or feels at this moment? What if you could let go of the idea that a deity is giving it to you or taking it away from you based on the notion that you are "bad" or "good"? This is NOT a rewarding/punishing Universe. This is a fast-moving, forward-expanding, unifying force for good and plenty! You can either be a part of it or resist it until you get sick and sad and falter—nothing can or will slow it down. You cannot be miserable enough to slow down a fast-moving train of abundance and alignment and amplification. You can't.

Ride the train and explore what it feels like to be limitless. You *are* that limitlessness.

Chapter 73

Metabolism

Your metabolism is energy burning through the body fueled by thoughts and emotion. Here's Google's definition:

1. the chemical processes that occur within a living organism in order to maintain life.

The Greek origin of the word meant simply to "change."

And so, if you struggle with your body's ability to process food into energy, there is still some part of you that is resistant to change.

Michelle did not want to hear this. We believe she is even getting a little angry with us for this suggestion, as she will tell anyone who wants to hear it how hard she works at maintaining her health through diet and exercise. As her weight has fluctuated throughout the years through her focus on fat or the lack of it, she wrote a "fiction" book, *All in Her Head*, about the process of loving herself through her obsession on a number on a scale (another man-made tool).

Right this moment, her weight loss has stalled at—get this—10 pounds above where she wants it to be to feel confident and to fit into all her clothes. And as she focuses more on the unwanted 10 pounds, those 10 could turn into 10 more, and 10 more...you get the picture! It's the power of 10 and the law of attraction working in the way that she does *not* want.

How does she change the flow of unwanted pounds? By halting the train of focus on the extra pounds and focusing on the way she will feel once she is at her desired weight—for Michelle—confident and light and healthy and energetic and having clothes feel good around her waist. This is the same way you create and manifest anything at all, you see. Focus more on what you want and how you'll feel when you get what you want than what is currently your unwanted reality, and watch how rapidly it will shift—and CHANGE!

As we told this to Michelle, the scale moved and she lost two more pounds without trying, just by her change in focus and perception. You can do this to add more weight and density to your body or to take weight away. As you shift your focus, you will naturally be drawn toward foods and movement that works for YOU—your soul, your body, right now—not those that work for all bodily forms, for you are all unique in your makeup. If someone offers a suggestion that "lights up" and resonates for you, try it out. If it makes you feel FANTASTIC, keep eating it and doing it! If it makes you feel "slow," perhaps it's just not for you.

No one can tell you which foods and exercise make you more energetic than your inner you. If you don't know what to eat, try meditating for a few moments before you shop or eat, and pay attention to what makes your mouth water. If you don't know what activities make you want to move your body, meditate and see what shows up on the blank slate of your mind. You could walk or run or dance or lift weights or hike or...do any of these options seem shiny?

If you were sick and on your death bed, what would your body want to do one last time before checking out? What does your soul long for on the physical plane? Then go do that, well and often, and forget about the number on the scale. It's only a number, and not representative of you in your entirety.

Chapter 74

Sensuality and Spirituality

Michelle had a dream a few nights ago where her former boyfriend, who is now deceased, came to her.

In life, this boyfriend had practiced lucid dreaming, where he could not only be cognizant within his dreams, he could enter Michelle's mind and detail her dreams. Michelle did not like it when he did this; she felt it was invasive and she told him so.

But now, after death, this boyfriend was entering her dream state in exactly the same way.

The interesting thing here is that Michelle awoke feeling quite sensual. *Not* sexual, as in the dream was not sexual at all. She sat with those feelings all day long and tried to figure them out from her analytical mind, which could not discern why.

Then she remembered how she'd been pondering in her meditations the feelings associated with the afterlife, the tangible emotions Michelle had felt in her near death experience decades before and that some friends had been asking about recently.

This former boyfriend was allowing her to feel what the afterlife is like from the relaxed state of her subconscious mind!

Let's define sensuality for you first, in order to grasp the enormity of what we are about to teach you. Google defines it as:

1. the enjoyment, expression, or pursuit of physical, especially sexual, pleasure.

2. the condition of being pleasing or fulfilling to the senses.

Please ponder the secondary definition. When you die, or we like to say graduate into the next dimension of your eternal existence, you will feel EVERYTHING—all at once!

Yes, it is indeed a sensory overload, but because you are not within the confines of a dense body, you can handle it.

You've been taught, according to your Bible, that sensuality is "lewdness" or "debauchery"—gratification of the senses to the exclusion of the soul and spirit.

We are here to tell you that it is the EXACT OPPOSITE! When you are pure soul as part of the greater whole of Spirit, you embrace all your senses at the same time! This is the ultimate gratification, and that is why you remain in a state of bliss.

The Bible is a very old book. There are some lessons to be learned from it, for sure, but they are not sound in your present evolutionary state of being. You are here to enjoy all of your senses, bodily and otherwise. When you pass, you will cherish the ability to *touch* while in a body, and so why not hug and kiss and hold hands with those you love and who love you back? Such expressions are made of Love, and you, too, are made of Love!

Of course, if another does not want your touch, you are not at liberty to touch them and must honor their boundaries. But if you share the same emotional vibrations of love and joy and trust and faith and loyalty and integrity and honesty, then by all means—SHOW IT.

Chapter 75

Processing the World Creatively

We have established that you are an active form of creation ever moving and evolving into more and better, yes?

We hope by now you have found outlets of creativity so you do not burst with stress and anxiety.

Michelle's writing is one way—her primary way—with which she processes the world at large. When she is happy and at peace, she writes, and when she is sad and angry, she writes.

Of course, now she allows us to write through her, but it is still a process of her mind seeking questions and for us to provide the answers through her body vehicle.

For others, you have your own way of processing the world and humanity, yes? Perhaps it's art, or music, or exercise, or designing buildings. There are many examples we could give here.

We want you to sit with the fact that if you are not currently processing creatively, you are likely processing destructively.

What does that mean? Your emotions need an outlet. When you are angry over a situation, if you do not let that anger out through a positive creation, you will eventually "let off steam" through an angry encounter that could result in violence, either through your words or actions. If you are sad, and you do nothing to alleviate the sadness, it will fester and eat away at your sense of self worth. Please look at why you are sad and angry—or whatever negative emotion you are feeling—and acknowledge it quickly before moving on and distracting yourself with something enjoyable and pleasurable. From there, create something.

You were born here to create! Not so much on other spatial dimensions, you see. But here on earth, you were meant to expand in material form through the energetic offering of your thoughts into matter. How FUN! Remember this? It's supposed to be *fun* here, and if you're not having enough fun on a regular basis, please change this.

Chapter 76

Approval

When you need approval you are asking the Universe to provide you with a void.

The hole that you feel is not real. You can make it real by your attention to it, but why would you do that?

The Universe, as we continue to teach, is ever-expanding and moving forward. Thus, you always have its "approval," because approval and acceptance are one and the same. The Universe doesn't hold an "opinion" about you or anyone else; the Universe is not a person and does not form thoughts.

If approval is the belief that something or someone is good or acceptable, or a good opinion of someone or something—as your Google defines it—then we say to you that because you are already Divine by virtue of being born, and because you are one with all of existence throughout more galaxies than you could possibly envision in one mind, then you really don't even need the word "approval" because you always already have it!

You are all connected, so if another does not see the good in you, they are really just not seeing the good in themselves. Shine your inner Light anyway, and they will perhaps see the same Light within themselves, or it will blind them by virtue of being too bright for their current vibrational reality.

When you die, when you graduate beyond this current level of existence, you will be able to handle the intensity of the Light. For now, it is only for some of you who are waking up to how powerful you truly are!

Some of you would say to embrace your "darkness," or your "shadow side," and we call that "folly." What you perceive as darkness is merely absence of your Light. You cannot "hug" something that is not there. Why not acknowledge when you are feeling low vibrationally and "fill up your cup"? It can be as simple as seeing that your vehicle's gas tank is running low, and going to the gas station to fill it up. This does not have to be an ordeal unless you make it so.

When your vibrational "tank" is low, do whatever you can to fill it up with pleasurable activities and service to others. Be kind. Give compliments generously and often.

Know that the inner "you" that you know as your soul stays "you" throughout all your lifetimes! Yes, you take on different "roles" in order to know the varied parts of your character and to recognize deeply how those roles do not even matter; they are just for fun and expansion! Live in integrity and honesty—and yes, transparency. Be fully *you* and others will respect your authenticity.

OR, alternately, they might challenge it. When you are no longer triggered by their accusations of whatever it is they seek in you that they do not see in themselves, you will know peace. And peace is what all of our teachings are ultimately all about. Peace is multifaceted, you see.

Michelle recently encountered a fellow "healer" at the collective in which she now hosts our circles. She was excited to see another woman who also did energy work and authored a book. They seemed to have some things in common, and Michelle has been setting the intention of allowing like-minded, like-vibing female friends into her inner circle and forming more positive, supportive, inspiring relationships.

But planning get-togethers with this person never seemed to work out (because when you are out of alignment with one another, that's what happens). When Michelle sat next to this person at a meeting, she felt as if something was amiss. She did not wish to feel this, and yet, there it was—a feeling of competitiveness and that this woman saw Michelle not as a friend, but as a "threat."

Michelle voiced this to another friend, and later got direct confirmation that her energetic suspicions were correct. The woman wrote to Michelle and confronted her with why she could not find our book listed as #1 anywhere online. Michelle told her she never said our book was #1 (yet) but that it was listed on several hot new releases categories which made it a bestseller. Michelle sensed jealousy, which was completely unfounded. (Our books then went on to hit the number #1 spot!)

Michelle felt anger! How dare this woman passive-aggressively suggest that Michelle was telling a lie? And how was it any of her business anyway?

Let's explore this at a deeper level.

The night before Michelle had gone to dinner with members of Jodah's family. No one mentioned the great success of our book, and Michelle felt sad about this, as she was quite proud. But when she brought it up, the family promptly changed the subject. Michelle felt crestfallen, as in the past, her birth family had a similar reaction.

Later, Michelle recognized this reaction as a need for approval, which was silly, you see, as the book being a bestseller was already evidence enough that *thousands* of people worldwide approved and accepted our book as being "good." But deep down, it revealed Michelle did not feel accepted as being "good" enough, a long-standing feeling of hers that was coming to the surface.

As she's writing this, Michelle is tearing up. It is her "shadow side" we spoke of earlier, and one many of you share, yes? It is okay, you see, to recognize it as so. At the same time, please promptly visualize pouring Light all over yourself, your inner you and the outer you—they are all one—and see yourself as the Light being who you TRULY are, without any darkness. You are "approved" of just by being here, you see. You made it! You made it out of the dark, created yourself from thought into form, and here you are, still creating. There is no finished "accomplishment"—your success lies in maintaining your high vibrational offering no matter what happens to you, and no matter what jealousies and insecurities exist in those around you.

You see, Michelle only attracted this "need for approval" because she was on the same vibrational "channel." Saying "rise" over and over again is a good way to regain her sense of self and to know where she currently is by what she is attracting to herself. This other person was merely reflecting back—in true holographic form—exactly what she was emitting! Now that she knows, Michelle has the option of changing her channel to a place that knows no suffering; that understands the purity of the soul that cannot do or feel or accept any damage.

Chapter 77

Horror

Michelle's daughter wanted her to watch a horror movie with her last night, even though Michelle didn't want to. Michelle complied to please her daughter, but early on she remembered why she does not like "scary movies," even when they are silly. She had nightmares all last night as the images played out in her subconscious mind. When she awoke, she said "rise" over and over again to lift her vibration higher in order to channel us today both in writing and in a radio interview.

Horror is defined as an intense feeling of fear, shock, or disgust. When you elicit those feelings, expect to attract experiences that reflect those lower-vibing emotions in your "real" life. Because Michelle is "sensitive" to such images and storylines, her body feels intolerant of them. There is already enough fear and shock and disgust in the world, don't you think?

And yet, her teenage daughter finds such movies a "thrill." It is not up to Michelle to convince her—or others like her—that their preference is "wrong." At the same time, we'd like you to ask yourselves in this moment what fears you are encouraging in your own life by choosing what types of entertainment and media outlets you watch and learn from?

You might think that these forms of entertainment are "harmless," but if they affect your frequency and adjust your state of mind, they are actively playing a role in your outcomes. Seek positive movies, books, and shows, and people that make you laugh, feel joy, and nod your head emphatically—and watch what happens! Your choices define your thoughts, actions, habits, belief systems, opinions, and so on. Your success is defined not so much by your accomplishments, but by how high you can maintain your vibrational offering in each moment. Ironically, as you maintain a consistent high vibe, your accomplishments will fall into place easily and with almost zero effort! Aim for the higher frequency, and all will come to you.

Aim for fear-based thrills and horrors, and you will attract more of the same toward you. If you find sad or even violent situations in your life, ask yourself what you're feeding your mind and perhaps make different choices.

Chapter 78

Still and Centered

You must remain in a still and centered state in order to "hear" the guidance you seek.

When you reject meditation as something else you "have" to do in order to feel happy and at peace, you resist the very clarity you wish to have.

If you can remain still and centered within a specific activity—such as yoga or a walk or a swim, or even cleaning your house or doing yard work—then the same guidance from higher vibrating souls may enter your consciousness, including that of your "higher" Self.

If you continue to struggle and suffer, as you have been taught to do, you will never know peace, and neither will the world join in on your peace.

Let us say LOUD and CLEAR: YOU ARE NOT HERE TO STRUGGLE AND SUFFER. Your suffering was part of an evolutionary maturation process in order to learn lessons in an expedient way. Now it has become a way of life for you—a "bad" habit, if you will, that it's time to break.

The less attached you are to your struggle, the less you will know pain. The less you know pain and heartache, the less you will suffer. The less attached to your suffering, the more you will know peace. And the more peace you feel on a daily basis, the more you will live out your Truth, which is bliss.

How many of you know bliss at this moment? Probably not a lot of you, or you are still likely experiencing moments of bliss or more evidence of pleasure that turns into a temporary state of happiness.

When you release your hold on your alleged "blocks" to bliss—STOP paying attention to them—they will dissolve into the nothingness they are. Keep telling yourself and others about all the blocks to your bliss, and they will continue to show up and get even BIGGER.

The only blocks to your bliss—and we've said this before, but it bears repeating—is your fear. Fear is attached to *this* realm, with its dense experience inside of a body. But your bodies will continue to change and grow lighter the more you hear our teachings and enact them from an inspired state—continue eating lighter foods and moving your bodies (and thus, inner cells and atoms) on a regular basis—and "make time" for being still and centered daily.

It is in the still and centered state that "magic" happens, where seemingly brilliant ideas enter the consciousness and your vibrational offering lifts, inspires, and enlightens! You don't have to "make time" for it. As we've pointed out, there's no such thing as "time." You only have to *want* to do it—to *be* it. Be centered and still today, and witness the outcome.

Chapter 79

Be Transparent

To be transparent means to be open and honest and 100% your self—your highest and best version of You—the soul that shines through the ages.

To be transparent means complete and utter intimacy with yourself and others, knowing you are one. It equates to authenticity, which you will find is highly regarded and relatable! So as you tune into this version of you, you will find that more and more people are drawn toward your Light, your Truth, and your immediate integrity.

What is immediate integrity, you ask? It's integrity in the moment—not after you have to think about it, you see. It's being *so* transparent that your reactions come automatically and not through a filter. The filter is good as long as you are learning tools on how to behave in the world and not act rude, selfish, or foolish. Once you move beyond the need for a filter, once you have read all our books and are meditating regularly and often, once you LIVE from a place of tender Love and all-encompassing compassion, you are ready to take the filter off and show your naked soul to the world.

Coming from this place will pose challenges, but you will be above them. Continue rising until you do, until you feel above all the lies, harshness, and judgment of those who share your earth. They may share your planet, but they do not have to make up your "world," your inner circle.

Keep those around you who are supportive and of a healing nature. If they are not, distance yourself until they return, or let them figure things out in their own circles. Rise, heal, amplify, give, be transparent. It will pay off.

Chapter 80

Either Way I'll Be Okay

Michelle and Jodah both are experiencing a lot of illness in different ways. Jodah has poison oak from hiking and a cold/flu that is making him tired and miserable, and Michelle is still having pain near her belly button that the doctors are not diagnosing. They know from our teachings that both ailments are forms of resistance, and that's okay.

Jodah doesn't want to work at his job anymore, but feels he still has to. And Michelle still fears "coming out" in a big way as her mother's influence still haunts her.

One is fear of the future, one is fear of the past. Both are illusions.

And yet, once an illness has found its way into the very density of the cells, it can take a while to undo the damage. Or not.

Time is not the obstacle, your degree of allowing the present good into your life is what matters.

If you can shift your thoughts toward the idea that no matter what unfolds you'll be okay—or in Michelle's case, no matter what has unfolded before—you'll move closer toward the space you want to be in order to heal and move forward.

Michelle feels there is a hernia in her abdominal wall, but the tests the doctors have ordered are not backing this hunch up. Her doctor is on vacation, so she must wait until he returns for a more definitive diagnosis.

Her well-intentioned friends are pointing fingers of blame that this is an emotional issue. But of course it's an emotional issue—ALL illnesses and ailments are! Mind your own business. Telling another the root of their emotional issues is righteous and ungrounded. It is up to each of you to figure out that you are Divine already—and not even "figure it out" as that would involve the mind and the analytical process.

A shift needs to occur in your energetic makeup—an allowance of Light in the soul throughout lifetimes of lessons. Come let it in…

We have told Michelle that either way she is okay. If she has surgery, she'll be fine. If she doesn't, she'll be fine. If you accept either direction, you'll always be okay, because you were okay before birth and you'll be okay after death.

BETTER than okay, you'll be phenomenal—you *are* phenomenal!

Stop attaching so much drama to the outcomes of your story, please. They are a made-up hallucination of the mind that has turned into matter within the very cells of your body. Change the direction of your thoughts by neutralizing them, and you win. When you win, we all win.

Jodah's situation is also temporary. He knows he will be fine, as it is just a cold and a rash and both will eventually go away with rest and fluids. Most situations turn out well for your body and mind with rest and fluids.

And if Michelle needs her belly repaired, that's okay, too. When your car needs a repair, you don't go searching for the emotional reason behind it; you just take it to the shop. (Update: Michelle has a congenital birth defect that caused an intestinal infection. A functional medicine doctor helped cure the infection and is treating the defect with herbal remedies.)

And so, if you find your body is ailing, and you know where the emotional component stems, honor the memory or the fear by naming it, then letting it go promptly before it does more damage.

If Jodah could flip-switch his thoughts toward those forward-thinking creative projects they are working on rather than his current job duties, he'd feel better immediately. And in that better feeling state, he'd attract more health, wealth, positive relationships, and opportunities.

If Michelle could let go of trying to please her "un-pleasable" mother, if she could feel worthy of all the good coming her way, her belly could shine bright and her digestive issues disappear overnight!

You still see such things as "miracles," and yet, we want this to become your everyday experience—shift your thoughts toward more and more of what you want rather than focusing on what you don't want. We'll keep saying this to you until you believe it fully.

Michelle took her dog outside yesterday and looked at the empty stand for a gazing ball she's never found. When they first moved to their house two years ago, Michelle searched for something to fit the stand that the prior owners had left behind, but couldn't find a beautiful one that fit the odd dimensions.

She thought, "I'd like to find a gazing ball for that stand. It would look beautiful in our garden during springtime." Then she let the thought go.

Later that evening, she went to a different drugstore for another item, and on a clearance table was a single, beautiful, odd-sized gazing ball for only $14.99 in all her favorite opalescent colors! Michelle bought it and took it home, and of course it fit perfectly.

We relay this story because it is an example of how things manifest quickly when you take it all lightly. In the case of a garden decoration, it can be rather simple to think a thought clearly then release it without desperation. Desperation works *against* manifestation.

In the case of bodily pain and suffering, the shift toward a state of wellness is more entrenched in suffering and desperation for relief.

If you are experiencing physical pain of any kind, see if today you might shift your thoughts and beliefs toward relief instead of desperation. Desperation fights the "current" of good-flowing thoughts and positive outcomes.

Say to yourself, "I now find relief. I feel relief by diverting my eyes and all my senses toward the beautiful. I feel relief by finding humor and experiencing laughter. I can laugh even when I'm in physical pain. Laughter heals. I now heal and find relief. In my relief, I find better feeling thoughts. In finding better feeling thoughts, I create better beliefs surrounding my path. In my best beliefs about my future and past, which don't really exist, I find Truth. In Truth, I experience faith and trust, and I know I am one with all that is."

Chapter 81

Detoxing from Drama

When you have been around—or created—a lot of drama in your midst, your body will feel it, if not now then later.

When you get so good at halting drama before it gains momentum, you will no longer experience the physical and emotional discomfort from it. You know the moment someone is being mean to you—or you are being mean to yourself through your inner critical voice—by the way it feels. If it feels intolerable, put a stop to it. Use your boundaries. Say—to yourself or to another—this does not feel good to me (what you're saying or doing), and I am holding the intention of only allowing thoughts and actions of support and well-being to filter into my daily existence, and so I need to move away from you for a while. Or you affirm to your inner self, "You deserve more than this behavior."

You may not choose to use those exact words, for it may feel cumbersome in this plane or in your culture. The point is, speak your higher Truth from your heart, affirm what it is that you *do* want in your life rather than what you wish to stop, and move away from the negative situation if possible. If it is your inner voice that is at issue, try replacing the negative thought with a positive one, as we have taught you in previous books, until you begin to think in affirmations rather than critical assessments.

If you've experienced drama and chaos, and you are now feeling the effects of it, you'll want to rest, renew, meditate, and bathe in pleasing encounters and situations until your vibe has lifted and left behind the traumatic memories of the experience. For in re-engaging in the "story" of what happened to you or around you, you are in effect re-igniting the same experience and bringing it into your present reality, over and over and over again. That will make you sick.

We will use for an example Michelle's recent hospital experience. She was going there to be healed from her acute physical pain, but the staff had nothing in their toolbox to offer her other than pain medications (which made her sicker) and more tests that came out negative. She persisted, trying to force the answer rather than practice radical acceptance of the situation she had somehow subconsciously caused.

In that use of subconscious force, she attracted several unpleasant situations with people who matched her lower vibe. The same ER doctor who had been on duty the first time she visited, refused to give her the CT scan her regular physician had wanted to see into her abdomen and check for a possible small bowel obstruction. The nurse could not start an IV because Michelle was dehydrated by now, and she called a bully nurse into the room and told her the patient was being uncooperative.

Michelle told them she wished to leave. They refused to let her, and so she tried to get out of bed and, because of her weakened state, fell. The nurse laughed at Michelle, and when Jodah told her to shut up, the bully nurse grabbed his arm and called security who escorted them both out to the parking lot.

This made an already low vibe situation even worse. They went to a new emergency room full of what seemed like hundreds of extremely sick patients in the waiting room. So they got back in the car, Michelle still in agony, and she stated the obvious: "We are in a low-vibrational frequency. Let's flip switch it. What do we *want* to have happen?"

And so, they began to state out loud the outcome they hoped for, that Michelle's former surgeon would somehow call her when they returned home and schedule a consult the next day and get the CT scan they wanted.

As soon as they got home, the surgeon's office called and did just that! But when they went to the appointment the next day, the surgeon was cold and apparently in a bad mood. She did agree to the test, but she said over and over again that there was nothing she could do.

In her weakened, sick state, Michelle was heartbroken at the surgeon's apparent lack of the compassion she had shown in the past. It was confusing, but Michelle held out hope that the new CT scan would reveal the answers.

The technician who treated her for the scan was kind, patient, and loving. However, this new scan still showed that there was absolutely nothing wrong with Michelle's body vehicle.

Michelle went home dejected at this news because she was in the mode of finding the answer, not seeing "nothing" wrong and still experiencing pain. She even yelled at us, letting us know that it's OUR body vehicle, too, and that we'd better do something! We laugh at this, not at her, but because she thinks it's up to us to do something for her, rather than lifting her vibration as we've taught her, and you all, to a place where answers are found and clarity achieved.

She gave up the struggle. In her fight for the answers, Michelle exhausted herself and fell into a deep sleep.

When she awoke, after a complete surrender, she saw a message from the owner of the healing space where we once hosted our Manifesting Miracles gatherings. She promised she could help Michelle, and at this point, Michelle had nowhere else to turn to in the western medical world, so she said yes.

Of course, the owner happened to be hosting a Reiki training at her center, and she could meet Michelle the next day during the break, even though it was a Saturday.

The healer held space for Michelle. She listened without judgment to her story, then assessed her bioelectrical field with a machine that printed out where there was weakness in the body. She then scanned the body using a magnetic resonance tool to make repairs accordingly, and gave Michelle supplements to assist in the repair. She showed her where there were emotional imbalances to address, gave Michelle a colonic—as her intestines were completely impacted and toxic—and insisted on doing all of this for free, because she heard in meditation that she was supposed to be of service in this way.

Now Michelle was overcome with gratitude and relief! Even though in the past she had been reluctant to receive such a huge gift, she simply said thank you and embraced this new direction, for it provided hope for recovery.

But after a day of following the new protocol, Michelle found her body was in heavy detox, sweating profusely and feeling ill and weak again. But now, she knew this was a temporary situation and could acknowledge the discomfort while raising her vibration in other ways.

In fact, we are writing through her now, for she has lifting her vibration to a place where we may reach her and flow through her.

We are not "doing" this to her. No one is. Michelle was in "making things happen mode" until she was *forced* to surrender and allow a better healing outcome, *which made its way to her*! This is what happens when you truly let go of an outcome, even while in extensive pain. The answers always align when you find relief from your suffering, when you "give up" the fight and energetically surrender and rest.

Michelle's friends keep telling her there's a lesson in this situation. And yet, we'd like to offer her some uncharacteristic advice here: don't try to figure out the lesson in your head. Your analytical mind does not know the answer. You may not find the lesson until you check out from this lifetime! Rest and let go, listen to music, observe beauty, talk to a trusted, supportive friend, and let the answers come to you.

We find it ironic that Michelle's CT scan had her filling up with "contrast" fluid in both her veins and through drinking it, so that the x-rays could show any possible blockages. Michelle was *literally* filled with contrast! And what happens after a lot of contrast shows up? A HUGE breakthrough is always the outcome. *Let* it come.

Michelle is detoxing from more than just the liquid contrast in her body vehicle, more than just the constipating medicines pumped into her body to avoid pain, she is detoxing from the drama in the hospital from people who were on a far different frequency than she is, even while she is in pain. Of course the pain and drama were intolerable! Now she must allow her body to do its job to restore the natural balance and harmony of its inner system. She must not interfere with this healing process by overthinking and analyzing its source. Instead, rest and renewal are in order.

This morning, Michelle and Jodah's propane ran out due to a faulty gauge. They literally have no power for cooking, showering, or heat. They must rest and renew—that is the vibe they've extended, and if they honor it, they'll see it's simply meant to be, and not a punishment or reward or anything like that. It's just time to heal.

Chapter 82

Scared Shitless

When we placed this thought into Michelle's head and she wrote it down for us, she laughed out loud.

Michelle is backed up, seemingly all throughout her intestines. She has been in her head, wondering why this is happening to her right when our second book in this series is about to be released. She is overthinking and analyzing the situation, thereby making it worse, despite all of our teachings of radical acceptance and faith and focus.

But we understand. Being confined within the density of a body is some heavy gravity, so we thought we'd lighten things up by pointing out that she is merely "scared shitless."

All of your body's illnesses, once again, could be attributed to resistance. We've said this before, but let's explore this further. What is resistance at its core? Resistance is fear. And so, all your illnesses can be traced to fear of some kind. And fear disappears entirely when you leave this dimension for others that don't require a bodily existence.

Please know this to be true: you have been in Spirit form more time than you've "owned"—more like rented—a body. And thus, you've been in a fearless state more than in a chronic state of fear of the unknown, yes?

Stop saying you're not in a chronic state of fear. You are, or your world wouldn't look the way it does now.

We are here to show you the way BEYOND the fear, a place of trust, joy, bliss, peace, and all desires fulfilled instantaneously—a place of no sickness, no violence, no worry, no stress, no pain whatsoever.

Please remember exactly who you ARE! You are this and more...get into the feeling state of your Spirit self and your fear can't reside there. Get into the feeling state of appreciation and gratitude for this very moment, and you can't experience fear at the same time! Fear and faith do not coexist in the same way that oil and water do.

Feel your way into faith. Know the fear is there—of course—or you would no longer inhabit a body! And yet, feel your way—through our various tools and heaps of meditation—into a place of trust and knowing all things are inherently for your greater good. All of it. Even the crappy parts.

Your poop, as Michelle's mind calls it, is representative of what you allow to process and digest while in a body. Michelle has struggled in the past with acceptance of a violent, negative, self-involved world that she feels every day, empathically. She has experienced a difficult childhood—as many of you have—and overcome it with a sense of compassion and courage. Lessons learned!

Even so, her body has stored her fear from long ago. Her intestines—just like your intestines—are several feet long.

Now you might point your finger right now at Michelle and laugh at her inability to defecate. And yet, where do you store your fear? Is it some other manifested form of illness, or do you defecate your fears all over other people? Does your fear keep you stuck in your life, frozen and unable to make a move from a mediocre existence to one that makes you feel ALIVE and spills over to help humanity?

Before you point a finger in blame and judgment, please reflect on where your fears show up. If you truly believe you're not experiencing any fears whatsoever, your life should be showing up for you as miraculous every single day. If you've reached that place, you wouldn't need to defend your alleged lack of fears. You would simply be basking in a Divine glow that would radiate without explanation. We hope that for you. We really do. But in order to reach that place while still in your body, you must stare your fears in the face and tell them to go away, because you KNOW who you truly are, and a Divine being knows no fears whatsoever—they just beam, like a star.

CHAPTER 83

Morals and Aspirations

You often assign a high title to your morals and aspirations, don't you?

What do we mean by that? You speak loftily about what your personal definition of ethics and morality is, which is nothing more than opinion formed from your belief systems that are formed from your society at large. Your beliefs are not always your own, do you realize that by now? What have you been fed, and what do you know for sure *right now*, in this moment?

The first definition of morals is, according to The Oxford Pocket Dictionary of Current English:

1. concerned with the principles of right and wrong behavior and the goodness or badness of human character.

As we have said, why is this *your* concern? Who decides what is right and wrong, good and bad?

Most of you would universally decide that killing is "bad," and yet you whole-heartedly agree to retaliate with killing en masse when war ensues, creating more killing in an endless cycle of useless corpses.

We have pointed out previously that you have all lived a great many lifetimes, yes? Lifetimes where you were both the "good," virtuous hero or heroine of your own storyline, and those where you weren't behaving so great, eh? You must have, by virtue of the sheer number of storylines you've designed, been a killer at some point, yes? In order to learn the lesson of NOT killing, of compassion, kindness, and unity, yes?

Those so-called "others" you point your finger at and judge are just playing out a "role" that you've assigned previously to your soul or you wouldn't be so outraged at their behavior. You recognize that that's a path that leads to suffering, and so you've evolved. But "they" are on a different path, on a different dimension, leading to the same "goal" of rising above suffering through faith.

That brings us to your goals and aspirations.

We might point out here that your goals are always a moving target while you are still in this earthly dimension. You thought that might be fun, given your perspective from where we are, a non-physical perspective where all is given at a moment's notice.

Within the density lies the challenge, and in spirit form, you must have been up to the challenge or you wouldn't be here.

To "aspire" means to direct one's hopes or ambitions toward achieving something.

And yet, please remember that the literary definition of the word aspire means to "rise higher." The origin of the word is "to breathe."

We've established the importance of your words to make thought into creation. Of course, this work is written in Michelle's native tongue of American English, and so as it's translated, you must come up with your own definitions based on where you originated or are currently located.

But as you stop getting righteous over what you deem right or wrong, *which does not exist in the afterlife*, please instead place your focus on your aspirations! **Breathe, and rise higher.**

In Michelle's home country her president, with whom she mostly does not agree, has declared war on another country that is already war-torn. Michelle is both sad and outraged, and yet, she can see many of her friends who agree that such violent action should be taken in order to stop further violent actions.

Do you see that you cannot "fight fire with fire," as your saying goes? In this case, fighting violence with more violence only escalates the focus on violence.

If you were to teach a child NOT to hit or hurt another, you would not hit or hurt them to teach a lesson, now would you? If you would, you need to go back and reread our other two books, for you have not evolved your soul to a place of peace.

You teach by example, always. Be a model of peace and understanding. Convey that peace and understanding through your words and actions, and eventually your world will be a beacon of hope and peace.

Notice we did *not* say your country!

You are ONE WORLD of humans, inhabiting a spinning globe of the same soil and water. Your national borders are manmade and inhibiting your progress as a species. When you speak to one another, speak *more* in terms of oneness than separation, and eventually your leaders will do the same.

Killing begets more killing. Period.

When will you stop killing each other? That is why we are here—to speed up the process of your evolution so you don't make yourselves extinct.

Or not. You may end up doing just that, and when you do, those of you reading these books will continue to soar in the great dimensional non-physical space where we reside, and that's not such a "bad" gig now is it? *We* enjoy it.

Chapter 84

Alliances

So how do you get through it? How do you get through a world of war and seemingly endless destruction and suffering?

Don't play your part in it. Unplug, as we have suggested previously. Do your part to "rise higher" each day, and you are doing far more than be enraged. Be engaged, not enraged! Engage in positive thought, positive interaction. Be kind and generous and loving, always. If you find a day when you are not bathed in such emotions, rest until you're there again.

Then join forces with like-minded, high-vibing "others" who are on the same path, the same wavelength as you—or maybe even a little higher! Form alliances of peace instead of resisting war, and you will know more peace, both individually and collectively.

Warmongers don't like it at all when you "unplug" from them. They thrive on the drama. Don't participate. Victims, too, thrive on the pain. It is *their* job to "rise higher," not yours. They won't listen to you until you yourself "rise higher." Then they just *might* pay attention, you see.

How you rise higher is by forming true alliances. You might have to go through a number of them before you realize they are true for you. People's energetic frequencies are always in a state of fluctuation, you see, and so those who might align with you at first might not a little later, and that's perfectly okay.

Re-align. Renew your aspirations, and continue to rise higher and higher, until it feels uncomfortable in your body's density. The body will adjust as the soul gets used to its higher standards of living.

The time is NOW. You *must* become a beacon of peace and hope, a "pillar" as you call it, so that "others" might see your strength and emulate it. We'll say it again: in Truth, there *is* no "other." You are indeed one. Please start acting like it.

How do you act like you are one, you ask?

By meditating more than reacting. By *knowing* that you can lend your energy to the collective consciousness that is waking up by your seemingly passive injection of peace. You may *act* from that space, if you truly feel called to action intuitively and are in a position of influence, but if you are not, either meditate until you rise higher, or pull yourself out of the game if you are enraged.

Your rage is unenlightened. Your anger may seem justified, but again, in the afterworld, there is no such thing. It is only here on earth where your fears and anger feel real, and we swear it's all an illusion. You will know and understand this when you leave this dimension, and yet, we want you to remember your many, many "times" between lifetimes where you knew this spiritual space, and can therefore recreate the feeling of it.

Please remember the time and spaces between lifetimes where you knew no such thing as anger or fear, as you were not within the confines of a body. Know that, and let it consume your current existence.

And keep going…

Chapter 85

You Are the Miracle

You are an experience in action—an original thought in form that is always in the process of recreating itself.

Therefore, who you are is always new again.

When you are feeling stuck and alone, stuck and afraid, stuck and allegedly "going nowhere," please understand that you are always going somewhere.

We've stated before that your cells are perpetually in motion, as are the planets in your galaxies. We, too, are in motion, at faster rates than your current mind can comprehend. As you transcend the dimensions, things and experiences will speed up, as will you.

For now, you must trust us that it is so.

Does this resonate at a deeper level? Does your soul know this to be Truth? Then act as if you are always in perpetual motion, and then those times of rest and renewal—when your body must repose in order to replenish—won't seem so heavy.

Continue to remember who you really are and the enormity of what you *did* when you created yourself by allowing the force of the entire Universe to run through your veins! In fact, you created your own veins, trusting that life-giving blood would flow through you to your organs without your even trying while you were still housed in a bodily form. Please remember now the miracle of your body that you wished into be-ing! You wanted it while still in Spirit, and there you have it, whether it is fully functioning right now or not.

Continue willing the body to recreate itself and it will. Stay stuck and it won't. It really is that simple. You want to live an amplified life? Then CHOOSE it! You want a grand purpose? Then DEMONSTRATE Love in its various forms! Create, move, be kind and generous, go out and wander. Trust that things will always work out because they always do, right? Perhaps not exactly the way you intended, but you allowed for some "wiggle room" as you moved into this thought-produces-form reality.

And thank GOODNESS for the wiggle-room, eh? What if all your thoughts became form instantaneously? From where you are currently, that could be disastrous. That happens for us from our non-physical dimension, and yet, we can just as rapidly redirect the creation because it is not a dense one. Matter can be tough to fix.

Tough, but not impossible. Nothing is impossible, right? You learned that from us.

CHAPTER 86

Healing Crisis

Innis

Crisis is what happens when existing beliefs run into—and perhaps clash with—emergent thoughts and desires. The old pushes against the new, thereby FORCING a release, which is why it doesn't feel so good.

A better way is to allow your new and approved pre-creations into your life in smaller, more digestible increments.

Michelle was asking why she keeps going through healing crises, and since I've been her "medical" and wellness guide from the beginning, she asked for me. I've been here as her spirit guide all along, and so now I'm here to share with you as one of The Power of 10, although we don't "see" ourselves as individuals any longer.

You could take this advice if your seeming "crisis" happens as a medical diagnosis, a relationship ending, a financial blow, or a career twist. Anything you deem "bad" you call a crisis; however, because there is no good or bad in our world, we'd like to point out to you how often a crisis precedes a big breakthrough. (Update: Michelle has experienced her huge breakthrough!)

Yes, we know we've taught you to learn through faith and not suffering. We know. And yet, your breakthroughs amplify your growth in a way that is currently needed, from a larger perspective of all humanity's point of evolution.

You have "midlife" crises, where the joke is a man trades in his practical car for a sportier, expensive one, and perhaps even goes so far as to trade his long-time wife for a much younger, energetic one.

The Truth is, you're always going through mini-crises, as a crisis could just be considered a really BIG change! And as we've pointed out all through this book—as well as the last two—change is a given. You wouldn't want things *not* to change, or you'd already have joined us.

The trick—and it's not really a trick at all—is to allow the change to happen, rather than to use energetic force. Yes, you understand physical force all too well, but the "trick" is to catch it before it turns into the physical.

Michelle's fears are old ones. She forgets just how much transformation she's been through—emotionally, physically, spiritually—in the past year as she's allowed us to talk through her to convey our teachings. It's only been a year.

And yet, she allowed us in, for which we are forever grateful. As her health improved prior to The Power of 10 entering her inner life, she "forgot" about me—her doctor in more than a few past lives.

As I've mentioned, I've been here all along, "waiting" patiently, as there *is* no real waiting where we reside. There is no sense of time—or space—because space is still a measurement of an unlimited source.

If you feel your spirit guides have abandoned you, know that's not possible. If they feel far away, it is only because your energetic offering has been altered to meet a new need—and therefore a new spirit guide more skilled in assisting you. You have no idea just how many of us there are!

Realize that there are almost eight billion people like you currently inhabiting the planet. There have been fewer, we understand, and yet imagine for a moment just how many souls make their transition each year. All of us here have made *many* such transitions, and have simply chosen a different path; one where we don't need to learn through suffering anymore.

As you experience pains in the body, understand that it is indeed a vehicle for the soul, which is the outlet for Spirit. The vehicle has wear and tear on it, yes, but it is also motivated by thought and inspiration, coming straight from Source energy. When you feel the pain, allow for it to show you the way—perhaps the healing "crisis" you face is actually a re-direct into something more and better!

Even if the healing crisis ends in the termination of this particular life story—this is HUGE, so please pay attention: you will STILL move into more and better, for you will enter into eternity, which you were always a part of…

You know this, but do you really LIVE as if you know it? If you did, you wouldn't fear death so much, you wouldn't fear and "fight" illness so much—what you "fight" expands also, so please stop fighting your pain or you'll make it much, much worse.

Allow the pain to meet you where you are and turn you toward the more expansive parts of yourself, those that know the Light and Love.

If it is a relationship crisis you face, the same goes. It is simply emotional pain you are in, rather than physical, and suffering—the attachment to your pain—is still completely optional.

Celebrate your transitions in life, for they are always offering you more and better, even if it doesn't feel so good in the interim.

Chapter 87

Self-service vs. Service of "Others"

Trubien

I am coming forward now because we are approaching the end of this particular book, and I would be remiss without speaking of service.

My name means "well-being," and as Dr. Innis spoke of healing, I will elaborate on the state of well-being. They are not the same, as you might have believed. Healing is the process of allowing your body to return to its natural state. Well-being is that natural state.

When you are in a state of well-being, you naturally want to be of service, for in serving others you are serving yourself, as in Truth, there is no "other." We hope you know that now, in the seat of your soul.

To be self-serving in your society has a negative connotation. The definition is:

    1. concern for oneself before others.

If you could know without a doubt that your Self is one and the same as the "other," you would give without measure, knowing it would return to you tenfold, as we keep teaching you.

You say you know this, but are you giving fully? What have you given today? This week? This month? This year?

Have you learned to manifest tenfold? If not, go reread book #1. Have you attained inner peace? Is your environment peaceful? If not, please go back and reread book #2.

Stop learning the hard way. There is a far easier path, one where you focus on the Truth we are pointing you toward, and release your attachment to suffering. As you do this, you will notice less pain, which creates even *less* suffering. And as you experience less pain and suffering, you will lighten your load, which is the true road to enlightenment.

You *can* attain enlightenment in this go-around—you CAN! We want that for you, all ten of us! And there are many more, you see. Billions of souls who no longer choose your dimension, because we've already done that and mastered it.

The ten of us simply decided to be of service through teaching, and Michelle allowed us the vehicle.

When she stops worrying about her vehicle, she will know health. As she knows health, she shall know well-being. And as her well-being spreads and she gives back, the world will know US. In knowing us, you will know each other as the one.

Chapter 88

Rally for Peace

Sofia

I have been with Michelle since the beginning. We all have, but I am the first one she "discovered" through her ample meditations.

I helped her write her first books because writing was my vocation throughout many, many lifetimes.

And now I am here to do more than just hold space for writing, although that is a great and noble method of delivering our messages to the world at large.

I am here to galvanize you into more and better, not just for you, but for ALL of you—meaning you personally as well as globally.

As we've mentioned several times, so many of you gather in resistance to something, and then you wonder why that "problem" escalates. You put all of your focus on the problem rather than the solution, and then the problem grows much larger.

Yes, unite! RISE, as we keep rallying you to do. And please practice the art and science of manifestation toward PEACE in the same way you've experienced it in the form of PLENTY.

In other words, rally together and state what you want, do not fight against what you *don't* want. The Universe "hears"—if the Universe had ears, which it doesn't, as we keep pointing out—what you DON'T want and adds to it, because you all share a positive, expansive, forward-moving creative Universe that "double-negates" what you are offering vibrationally.

What does that mean? It means that a negative times a negative always equals a positive in mathematics, yes? And in the same way, when you focus AGAINST a negative outcome, the Universe ignores the "negative" and puts it into positive, forward-moving language that registers with its frequency. It cannot vibrate with violence, for example, for that is such a low-vibrating action caused through repetitive emotional obsession with anger, fear, and regret that it simply cannot "register." The energetic difference is just too vast.

And so, I encourage you now to rally together in peace. Advocate what you want, and do it together. Meditate individually, and also in large groups. People will take notice of your sitting together in peace, and they will feel your peace, and your peace will AMPLIFY and serve as an example to all of what can happen energetically when you focus—with the flow of the entire Universe in you and around you—together in unison.

Host "Peace is Power" rallies! There are many definitions for your word "rally" and yet we would like you to note the French origin, meaning to "bring together again."

Assemble in mass meetings, yes, and emanate your Truth! Don't just speak because words are limited. You know the saying, "Be the change you wish to see in the world." That is how you do it. Be the change. Meditate together in public, let it go "viral," let it "trend," as you say.

Never before have you been this powerful together. The internet has served as a medium for you to unite, if you so desire. Your social media has been used to polarize as well, and to attempt to build fear and resistance. But I am here to RALLY—as in cheer—you on to your

Divine inherited GREATNESS through raising your vibration and sharing it with a mostly "sad" world.

Think of The Power of 10 as your personal pep squad, cheering you on, building you up, synchronizing your energies up to our spiritual reality—YOUR eventual reality, once you know the Truth.

I am here because Michelle is feeling triggered by the fear of war in her country. Within the past week alone, the president of her nation has sent an airstrike to Syria, allegedly in retaliation to their leader's violent acts against "his" people. He is also threatening North Korea, who is still doing nuclear testing, and has been for years. Her leader has sent war ships to the area, and China is backing North Korea.

When Michelle was a little girl of 10, she learned in school of the first nuclear bombs that dropped in Hiroshima, and it made her ill for months. She had nightmares of the aftermath, of people missing limbs and dying/dealing with nuclear fallout sickness.

Now, with all these threats looming and a seemingly mentally unstable president at the helm, her dreams are returning. She fears World War III.

Michelle must STOP her fears before they join forces with other fears of war and turn into a horrific reality! Your thoughts become things, both individually and collectively. And so, it is IMPERATIVE at this time that she—and YOU—turn your thoughts to a world that lives harmoniously, of shining LIGHT on your unstable leaders around the world so that they do not "fight fire with fire," but counteract violence with peaceful negotiation, leading by EXAMPLE.

You would not spank a child to teach them not to hit, would you? If you do, STOP. You are teaching via a "double negative"—as we spoke of previously. In this example, you are showing others violence to teach non-violence and these negate each other. In the same way, do not kill others as a way to teach NOT killing. Do not argue against war torn nations by tearing them apart with more war and violence and killing.

It is insanity.

Peace is invisible, but it is *felt* by the heart and soul. The actions of war and violence are visible in your dense reality, and therefore gather more reaction. Instead of feeling and acting on a reactive thought, try sitting with it, then flip-switch it toward thoughts of peace. Again, what would a peaceful world LOOK and feel like to you? What if there were no national borders, because in Truth there are not. What if there were no nationalities, because in Spirit, there are none.

It's time to speak more of your shared ONENESS than your illusionary differences and man-made separationist stories.

RISE UP.

What does that mean? It means you lift your vibrations daily, as we've offered you in this book and the prior two. It means you share your vibrational frequencies with "others," knowing your higher energetic offerings are contagious in a good way. You go out into the world with your higher energies, not blocking the "bad," not "showing off," but SENDING OUT your higher vibes so that others may be inspired by your Light and shine their own.

When a negative mood strikes, take yourself "out of the game" through rest and renewal. Spend time in the natural beauty of your environment, and come back to re-engage for peace.

Travel often and well, so that you may know that cultural differences are learned behavior, and you share more as human be-ings—as souls united in Spirit—than you detract in your made-up differences as a species.

Your religions are man-made and made up. Your politics are man-made and made up. Let go of the stories behind what you think you know. You know nothing, and yet, you contain all of life itself.

You become ONE WORLD when you speak more of your present peaceful reality than your cultural heritage.

Tear down your walls and you will know intimacy. Love one another, and know the love that is within you at all times. Fear nothing, as the "worst" that can happen to you in the dense lifetime is that you go back to the "drawing board" and you either create a new life story or move BEYOND into higher realms of bliss.

The gateway to BLISS is PEACE, and so peace is what we are offering in this book.

Peace is something you can know in each moment of every day. Take notice of your peace, and it shall grow and spread. It is who you are after death and between lifetimes and beyond this dimension.

CHAPTER 89

On Purpose

Gil

When you do something by accident, you often say that you didn't do it "on purpose."

I am here to teach you how to always do things "on purpose," so there *are* no accidents any longer.

When you set the intention to act "on purpose," or act "as if" you already are the Divine be-ing that you want to be (you are!), or act as if you already have the thing you want (you do!), you are enacting your purpose, which is to be in service of the Love that you contain.

At nearly every seminar we host, we hear this question: "What is my purpose?" So often you tie this to a job choice or a career, and while that certainly could be fulfilling, you'll discover when you cross into the next dimensions that it didn't serve anything at all other than to pay your bills and "buy time," which can't be bought, because it doesn't exist. (To learn more, please visit **www.YourLifeRepurposed.com**)

You are here to do far more than "pass" the time and live out a mediocre and unfulfilling existence! You are meant to THRIVE, to enact each moment with deliberate intention...ACT with clarity and you'll gain it, not the other way around—as in, asking for clarity as if it's not already right in front of you.

You gain clarity and direction by living it out, by your non-reaction to events in your world that seem unsettling, because you know it's all just an illusion now, a game. As you live in certainty that everything is always moving you forward toward your best and highest Self, those "mistakes" will stop occurring, because you'll stop living by "accident."

This does *not* mean you will *not* be in a state of allowing; that's a double negative, but you know what I mean, don't you? Once you are certain that life is for you rather than against you, you will automatically be in a state of allowing all your good to flow through you because that is the natural order of things.

The only thing that ever disrupts the flow is your resistance and negativity.

Please notice when your body is tightening up, as if preparing for war. Does your jaw clench when you don't like something the way it is? Do your shoulders hunch up? Does your stomach tighten, your forehead wrinkle? Your body is telling you that you need to relax into the flow, to trust, to surrender, to have faith. Breathe and let go, breathe and let go—say it with me, "Breathe and let go."

The more you say this to yourself, the easier life on earth will get. And in time—your lifetime now—you will reach the way station, and beyond to where we reside as we so choose.

You can count on us, you know. You can ask for guidance, from us or others who've chosen not to return to a lifetime of suffering and lessons, who are bathed in the Divine Light where you came from and where you'll go. As we've all said, you have been more often in that unconditional Love and Light than you have in your lifetimes.

We are here for you, you just need to ask. You may not see or hear us, as Michelle does, but you can feel our presence and allow it to envelop you. That may be all you need to lift your vibrations, and lifting your vibrations leads to health, wealth, wisdom, and relationships.

It's time, now, for you to *direct* your vibrations EVEN HIGHER—to skyrocket them forward into the atmosphere, where "you" belong—

the many yous that exist all at once, at least. Your body is here, but your soul can travel anywhere it wants while tethered to the body. Let it go. Let it travel outward to connect with your true Divinity—it should feel blissful and amazing! If it doesn't, if you are too identified and attached to your body, you're simply not ready. If you feel unsettled, go ground yourself with the methods we've taught in our last two books. Take your shoes off, walk around the dirt. Shower, bathe, swim. Connect with the earth, then re-connect with Spirit.

Our purpose is now your purpose, you see. Our purpose was to come here collectively to teach you how to reach higher, to know more and to "do" less, to live amplified and expanded…are you there yet? Probably not consistently, and that's okay. Keep reading, keep practicing, keep meditating, and you'll get there. Use the gift of your ample powers of imagination, and step away from anyone who tells you to get "realistic." This is indeed realistic, as it's in your power to create an amplified state of be-ing!

When you find yourself telling a story about how you or someone you hang out with isn't doing things "on purpose," or that they have "good intentions" that their actions aren't demonstrating, please ask yourself why you're covering for them—or for yourself? Commit to your path, and you'll see evidence of progress—you'll feel it. If "others" truly do have positive intentions, it will show. If they do not, their actions will show you where they are, and you have the choice to step away and find your supportive, uplifting tribe—ALL of whom are living a life "on purpose."

When you gather and live and engage in this way, your life will feel FULL! Maybe not complete, because then it would be time to "go" and move on to the way station. Let it feel full to overflowing, enjoy the beauty of your world, then move toward us when you do feel complete.

Chapter 90

Peace Party

Laurel

I realize that Sofia just spoke of peace "rallies," but I would like to take a different tack, one that is less serious and more fun.

The basics of manifestation teach that you act as if you already have what you want, because you do in other dimensions. We've taught you this, and as you practiced it, you hopefully found the feelings of having what you want. And the energetic vibrations of those emotions brought it to you—the thing or experience, that is.

It's not "magic" per se. Although it may feel that way! "Others" who do not understand the way things work may call it that, as anything people don't understand they tend to label as "magic" or "crazy."

There is nothing crazy about allowing your creations to happen in the physical world. In fact, the more they do so and show up as "evidence," the more you will have to demonstrate and lead by example.

And as you do so, again, as all the great manifestations of your life begin to "pile up" and spill over and out unto the world, it's time to connect the same tools with amplifying peace on your planet—for without peace, you have nothing.

So instead of holding a big rally—or perhaps in addition to hosting one—hold a smaller "peace party" in your home or neighborhood. Celebrate peace—act "as if" you already live in a harmonious world that works together instead of against itself—and you will see more evidence of it daily! Feel the emotions of living in a world without violence, a world of cooperation and unity, where everyone's basic needs are met and health challenges are overcome with ease, and you will indeed live in THAT world! Celebrate peace as if it's already a reality, and it will become one.

Who doesn't like a reason to celebrate? You'll gather more people toward peace if you make it a party instead of a rallying "cry," although Sofia's rallies are definitely "on purpose." Just don't make it a "cry," or you'll turn yourselves into victims.

We want for you to be the opposite of victims—be champions! Be champions of peace, and you will celebrate each and every moment you're experiencing this life as you know it.

Conclusion

All of Us—as One

Make no mistake—make LOTS of them!

If you look over your lifetimes from our expansive perspective, you'll see clearly that everything happened the way it was supposed to. Everything that has ever happened to you happened FOR you.

You've learned so many lessons you've lost count. Stop trying to remember what you came here to learn; it's there, safe inside your soul, which is infused with Spirit.

Your "work," if we may call it that for a moment, is to let go. Let go of control, let go of perfection. Release all worry—not to God, for we've established God is not a person. Just let go—period. Release and let go, over and over again—maybe say it aloud until you feel the way you wish to feel, all the time.

When you "give it to God," you might be disappointed when doing so didn't teach you what you needed to learn. If you give it to "God," which is Love, know that God or Love wants you to be more like Love. If you feel too far away from Love, let go until you feel its return, for Love has never left you, you just forgot you were It.

There are no mistakes, and the only guarantee is that after you leave this little lifetime, there will be more...and more and more and more! The only sure thing is that there will be nothing at all to forgive, for you came here to expand all of consciousness forward through your creations from thought into form. The only reality is that you will return to your original form—which is not form at all! Without form, you will truly know the expansiveness of the Universe, for there is not a body to hide behind, not a mind to hide within.

Tap into some of that expansiveness now, and amplify it tenfold, and you will lead an amplified life! How will you know how this feels?

Let's start here: when you make "mistakes," you will laugh at them, for you know what they point toward. When you do that which feels good to you, you will connect with the same energy fields that continue to create forward-moving growth, into an eternity that knows no bounds.

You are almost there. We feel it now, and it satisfies our united soul.

We'll talk soon...

With Amplified Love,

The Power of 10

About the Author

Michelle Paisley Reed is an international #1 Amazon bestselling author, inspirational speaker, and spirit channel. She's written four screenplays and six books (and counting), including the first two in this series, *Manifesting Miracles and Money: How to Achieve Peace, Purpose, and Plenty Without Getting in Your Own Way*, and *Peace is Power: A Course in Shifting Reality Through Science and Spirituality*.

Other books by Michelle include: the non-fiction sensation *Yoga for a Broken Heart*, *All in Her Head*, and *All Over It*.

A new reality TV show, "Don't Change The Channel," is currently in development, and she is featured in the Australian film/TV show, "The Difference." Michelle is a former news journalist and lives with her husband, 10 spirit guides, a dog, and two cats in Northern California.

CONNECT WITH MICHELLE & THE POWER OF 10

Website: www.WeAreThePowerOf10.com
Facebook: www.facebook.com/WeAreThePowerOf10
Instagram: www.instagram.com/wearethepowerof10
Twitter: www.twitter.com/wearepowerof10
Pinterest: www.pinterest.com/powerof10

Join The Power of 10 "High Vibe Tribe" in our private Facebook Group:

   www.facebook.com/groups/PowerOf10HighVibeTribe

When you're ready to shift toward a life of FREEDOM, please visit:

   www.YourLifeRepurposed.com

Other Books by Michelle Paisley Reed

Manifesting Miracles and Money: How to Achieve Peace, Purpose, and Plenty Without Getting in Your Own Way

Peace is Power: A Course in Shifting Reality Through Science and Spirituality

Yoga for a Broken Heart: A Spiritual Guide to Healing from Break-up, Loss, Death or Divorce

All in Her Head

All Over It

BOOK DISCOUNTS
& SPECIAL DEALS

Sign up for free to get discounts and special deals on our best selling books at

www.tckpublishing.com/bookdeals

www.ingramcontent.com/pod-product-compliance
Lightning Source LLC
Chambersburg PA
CBHW070051080526
44586CB00013B/1014